JOB CREATION

*How It Really Works
And Why Government Doesn't Understand it*

David Newton

Andrew F. Puzder

E³ FREE MARKET PRESS
SANTA BARBARA ✛ CALIFORNIA

Copyright © 2010 by David B. Newton - All Rights Reserved.

Printed in the United States of America. Except as permitted under the United States Copyright Act of 1976, no part of this publication may be reproduced or distributed in any form or by any means, or stored in a data base or retrieval system, without prior written permission.

ISBN: 978-0-615-43635-7

JOB CREATION

Table of Contents

Acknowledgements	4
Introduction	5
1 - Entrepreneurs, Innovation, and the *Invisible Hand* in the US Economy	20
A Crash Course in American Private Enterprise	22
Ideas Create Companies That Create Jobs	30
The US Economy's Resilient Track Record	32
2 – 100 Years of U.S. Employment: 1910-2010	36
A Crash Course in American Employment	37
Focus on the Last Decade	46
The Certainty Factor	53
3 - How the Private Sector Views Job Creation	56
Capital and Labor, Supply and Demand, ROI	58
Marginal Productivity and Economies of Scale	64
Hiring and The Certainty Factor	65
4 - How the Government Views Job Creation	68
Nothing Created, No Benefits Accrued	69

JOB CREATION

Stimulus and Federal Healthcare Don't Work	73
Disregarding the Certainty Factor	79
5 - Wealth Creation vs. Wealth Redistribution	83
Lessons From Frank Knight	84
Wealth Creation-Redistribution Gap	85
Crippling the Certainty Factor	91
6 - Primary Job Creation: The New Hire	95
Hiring Is A Business Decision	96
Value-Added to Companies and Employees	108
The Certainty Factor In Action	112
7 - Secondary Job Creation: The Ripple Effect	117
The Employment Multiplier	118
Proximate Job Creation	122
The Geometric Certainty Factor	126
8 - Great Examples Politicians Can't Understand	131
Business Models and Job Creation	132
Billion Dollar Corporate Model	137
Entrepreneurial Start-Up Model	145

JOB CREATION

The Certainty Factor and Business Models	147
9 - A Straightforward Plan for Job Creation	151
Lessons From Jeff Foxworthy Fifth Graders	153
Stop Creating Fear and Uncertainty	156
Four Proposals for Job Creation	163
Reduce Taxes, Overhaul Simplify Compliance – Increase Certainty	164
Conduct a Cost Benefits Analysis to Eliminate Regulations That Impede Economic Growth – Increase Certainty	173
Dramatically Cut and Limit Government Spending – Increase Certainty	182
Expand All Segments of Domestic Oil – Increase Certainty	187
Realistic Projections of Increased Certainty	191
10 - Added Perks of Successful Job Creation	198
More Tax Revenues: Lessons from Laffer	198
More Capital and Lower Costs of Capital	204
Even More Jobs	206
Conclusion	211

Acknowledgements

We want to say thanks to our many colleagues and business associates who have provided strong support and encouragement for this entrepreneurial endeavor.

Special thanks go to Westmont Student Research Assistants, Alexandria Sumner and Danny Price who provided a wealth of periodical research that contributed greatly to the final manuscript, and to Eric Knopf and Vision Launchers for the great design work on our webpage and cover artwork.

Good Venturing!

JOB CREATION

Introduction

*"The role of government is to stabilize and then
get out of the way as quickly as possible.
Ultimately, the recovery will be led not by the government
but by industry, business, and the creativity,
ingenuity and enterprise of people.*

*If the measures you take in responding to the crisis
diminish their incentives, curb their entrepreneurship, and
make them feel unsure about the climate in which
they are working, the recovery becomes uncertain."*

- Tony Blair
Former British
Prime Minister

It may seem strange to introduce a book about job creation with a quote from the former leader of Britain's Labor Party, but experience is the most effective of teachers and Prime Minister Blair appears to have learned his lessons well. His commentary is piercingly insightful while remaining elegant in its pure simplicity. We heartily embrace these words as a clear synopsis of the pathway out of our current economic malaise – with one clarifying addition to his last four words. Yes, we agree, government will not lead the recovery. It never does. Instead, an unencumbered private sector of companies and individuals can - and will - lead the recovery, but they must have a strong degree of *certainty* about the positive prospects for being creative, innovative, enterprising, and profit seeking. Blair rightly understands that

JOB CREATION

given our current economic malaise, the Obama Administration's actions to-date are set to actually diminish wealth-creating incentives, curb entrepreneurial new ventures, and make the private sector increasingly unsure about the future economic climate in which it will operate. If that is the case, any opportunity for recovery and robust job creation not only becomes more <u>un</u>*certain*, but it plainly and simply *will not happen*. A sustainable recovery requires strong corporate profits, a balanced budget with drastically reduced government spending, reduced business regulation, and across-the-board lower individual and corporate taxes. These will release the U.S. free enterprise system's dynamic energy for growth, incentivize entrepreneurship, and lead to robust job creation - THE key indicator of any economic recovery.

Since the financial collapse of 2008 and the recessionary contraction that followed, the headlines have bemoaned the reality that over $800 billion of federal government "stimulus" programs have done nothing to set the U.S. economy on course toward a sustained recovery and robust job creation. Even as we make final edits to this book in early December 2010, the unemployment picture has been consistently disturbing for months. The September 12th cover of the Los Angeles Times reported: *"America Out of Work: Ugly Reality Looms for Job Seekers"*, noting: "It could be years before the labor market recovers [and] many will run out of benefits long before that" (www.heraldonline.com/2010/09/12/2444563/ugly-reality-looms-for-job-seekers.html). Now three months later, the December 4th Los Angeles Times front page article is: *"U.S. Unemployment Climbs to 9.8%, Raising Doubts about Recovery."* As the article concludes: "All that points toward the prospect that high unemployment levels could stretch much further into the future than most economists had expected" (http://articles.latimes.com/2010/dec/04/business/la-fi-jobs-20101204).

In one way, both articles are absolutely correct. If the current administration continues its present course of massive federal

JOB CREATION

spending programs, increased taxation, more business regulations, and greater intrusion into the lives of private sector companies and individuals, the "ugly reality" will then be President Obama's disastrous legacy of failed policies and misunderstood American private enterprise. The economic uncertainty introduced by this administration's disdain for corporate profits, its love affair with trillion-dollar plus budget deficits and out of control federal spending programs, its pursuit of broader business regulations, and its promise of higher individual and corporate taxes, together create huge disincentives against economic growth that ultimately kill job creation and maintain high unemployment.

During any economic crisis - and the current crisis is certainly no exception - the job creation debate is all about confirming or rebutting whether government intervention with stimulus programs can actually help the economy by creating sustainable jobs, or whether government should reduce spending, reduce business regulations, cut taxes, and allow the private sector to create sustainable jobs. While this may sound like a worthwhile intellectual inquiry into competing economic theories, any actual competition of ideas is all but nonexistent. In reality, the national debate over how to create new jobs is plainly and simply NOT at all a legitimate debate. A meaningful debate requires two or more viable positions from which to address a given issue. Some baseline level of reasonable feasibility for a given position - albeit perhaps only remotely likely - serves as its entry pass into such a forum of ideas. How that position fares once admitted to the formal exchange of argument from all sides, is then subject to the strength of its tenets, the clarity of its expressed rationales, and the substance of its content in capturing the hearts and minds of its counterparts, as well as the gallery of onlookers. What makes the issue of job creation so unique is that there *literally* are no second, third, or "other" viable positions from which to logically, meaningfully, or intelligently engage in this debate. Only one position has secured that requisite level of reasonable feasibility with empirical evidence that is consistent and overwhelmingly profound. The sheer volume of data covers more than 100 years of American history. Its inherent *veritas* provides it exclusivity into the debate arena, rendering all other prospective rationales and positions immediately, definitively, and permanently excluded from formal consideration. *Private enterprise, unencumbered by excessive government intervention, will create jobs. Period!*

Throughout this book, we will focus on *The Certainty Factor* and how it is the primary catalyst for sustainable job creation. While we will discuss it in greater detail in Chapter Two, *The Certainty Factor* captures whether individuals and businesses throughout the private sector are ready to take risk – to invest, remodel, expand, modernize, borrow, purchase, and hire – based upon their collective perceptions and expectations about the certainty (or uncertainty) of the economy in the future. Quite simply, greater certainty creates positive expectations that are then the catalyst for productive economic action, while greater uncertainty creates negative expectations, which result in little or no action in the private sector. This uncertainty translates into a stark reality, namely, that businesses and individuals are less inclined to (or simply will not) utilize their cash to expand, modernize, make new purchases, and hire new workers.

For example, let's apply *The Certainty Factor* to our current economic crisis. It's noteworthy that heading into the last four months of 2010, "American businesses are sitting on top of a record $2 trillion in cash reserves - money that could be spent hiring more workers, funding new projects, or paying out dividends to investors; but right now these dollars remain stuck on the sidelines, as businesses of all sizes [try to assess the] five main costs that impact their bottom line, [and] thanks to the agenda in Washington, all [five] are going up, turning the White House's much-touted 'Recovery Summer' into the "Summer of Uncertainty" (Eric Cantor, *Beware of the Obama Tax Increases,* USA TODAY, Sept. 3, 2010, http://www.usatoday.com/news/opinion/forum/2010-09-02-cantor01_ST_N .htm). Clearly, no economy

JOB CREATION

ever needs the greater uncertainty and negative future expectations that come from higher taxation, increased federal spending, and further government intervention into the private sector. Lower taxes, reduced federal spending, and less government intervention would reduce future uncertainty, raise positive expectations, and result in significant economic action within the private sector. One of the principal results of this positive economic certainty would be robust job creation.

So why then do federal, state, and local politicians continue to ignore the preponderance of supporting facts for how to create jobs, as they continue to roll-out supposedly "new" proposals, programs, and awkward spending initiatives they believe will add to national employment? Such policies actually erode - and eventually destroy - *The Certainty Factor.* The result is <u>in</u>action by businesses and entrepreneurs inevitably leading to higher unemployment and its parallel economic contraction. Quite simply, if job creation and economic prosperity were a result of government action and stimulus, currently we should be experiencing one of the greatest economic booms in our history. Congress and the Obama Administration have poured trillions of dollars into the economy with stimulus spending, loan guarantees, housing tax credits, and cash for clunkers (among many other things), while for two years the Federal Reserve has held interest rates near zero. Despite an increase in unemployment and lackluster economic growth, defenders of this absurd policy can only offer the speculative and severely challenged explanation that things *would have been* worse, had it not been for all this government involvement and stimulus spending. Surely, even they must know this is ridiculous.

The unfortunate reality is that such federal spending initiatives are actually more intended to expand the power and influence of government than to improve the economy and create jobs – as many politicians actually believe a bigger government is better for the economy and society in general. In either event, our current

JOB CREATION

administration and lawmakers are perplexed that their invasive policies, regulations, and higher taxes have failed to spark job creation, and have actually reduced new jobs, while raising unemployment and racking up massive government debt, with significant inflation soon to follow. They are committed to the ideal that a more powerful federal government is better able to solve our economic problems than the free enterprise system of entrepreneurial initiatives that built this great American economy in the first place. Of course, the individuals making this determination are the same ones who hold those government positions, and whose personal power will be enhanced by expanded government control over our economy and our lives.

We believe this is absolutely the wrong course to pursue, as proven emphatically by both history and common sense. Rather, the remedy for this current economic malaise is to do everything to bolster *The Certainty Factor,* which will develop strong positive future expectations, allowing entrepreneurs and existing companies to seize the economic opportunities of our free market, which will then generate economic growth and create a wide range of new jobs that are necessary to restore prosperity. The simple fact is that the private sector can and will create the jobs necessary for the economy to recover IF the government will allow it to function at its full potential. The government, on the other hand, is incapable of creating the sustainable jobs necessary to lift us out of our economic troubles. In fact, its efforts to do so, while attempting to direct and regulate the private sector, have already both prolonged and exacerbated the problem.

Rather than adhering to *The Certainty Factor*, many among the political elite are persuaded by Keynesian economics and its reliance on government spending and centralized planning. Yet, the Keynesian school has convincingly proven itself both historically and logically to result only in sustained economic decline. Rational individuals should finally and formally relegate such schools of thought to banter and informal small talk, yes even

JOB CREATION

mere *chit-chat* among those political elites wandering the corridors outside the official debate arena, as they lack even the most fundamental logic or bases to merit admission to reasonable dialogue. As such, their proponents need to accept their collective resignation that nothing they propose has any credibility, or lends anything meaningful to the global, national, industry, or firm-specific discourse about job creation.

Socialist governments' manipulation of various economies has fared so poorly over the decades in the times it has previously been admitted to the formal exchange of argument, that its weak tenets, unclear rationales, and lack of any substantive positive results have failed to capture the hearts and minds of its counterparts (let alone the collective national gallery of observers), while continually leaving all audiences in wonder, disbelief, and amazement that anyone could *ever* take their line of reasoning and proposed outcomes seriously. In fact, most Americans do not support the big government, big spending schools of thought. In a Rasmussen Poll taken in July of 2010, 75% of likely voters (three out of every four Americans) preferred a free market economy to a government-managed economy, while just 11% (only one in nine) preferred that government should manage things. Despite 18 months of aggressive government action, 69% (essentially seven out of every ten) preferred *more* competition and *less* government regulation - compared to more regulation and less competition - for improving the economy and creating jobs. Only 19% (less than one in five citizens) preferred more government regulation and less competition. Yet, the current political elite preferred a government-managed economy over a free market economy, but by only 44% to 37% while, among mainstream voters, 90% (nine out of ten, or NINE times as many) preferred the free market, and this preference was found across all demographic and partisan lines.

This highlights perhaps the most surprising aspect of the current job creation discussion, namely that those serving in government,

JOB CREATION

just don't get it! Grasping *The Certainty Factor* presented in this book is completely foreign to them. The main reason for this is that most politicians have never started or run a private sector business. Many have never even had a job in the private sector, outside of government or politics. They are literally unable to comprehend how American private enterprise really works. They certainly fail to grasp the fundamental tenets of basic macro- and microeconomics, accounting, finance, marketing, sales, and operations. They have a pervasive ignorance of the private sector's incredible potential to create jobs, and government's inability to do so meaningfully.

For example, the September 21, 2009 cover story of *TIME* magazine stated: "Out of Work in America: Why Double-Digit Unemployment May Be Here To Stay – And How To Live With It." That tone and perspective define the political class. The cover shows thirty jobless Americans from Atlanta and San Francisco. And while the headline connotes the hardship of the recession, the subtitle first plants the seed that over 10% unemployment could become a fixture of the US economy (here to stay?), but then offers inferred hope that readers can learn to accommodate this supposed new reality with a few simple tactics for enduring economic pain. It is difficult to imagine a more short-term and out-of-touch perspective, or one that is more clearly in direct conflict with *The Certainty Factor* covered in this book. In the past 100 years, double-digit unemployment occurred only during the Great Depression (1930-1940) - before America entered WWII. And that's it! Yet *TIME*'s cover-story author -J.C. Ramo - clearly suggests that the US economy is now once again in "great depression" mode, and likely will be so for quite some time. While this is certainly a possibility, it is *only* a possibility if the government remains committed to over-regulating, over-spending, and over-taxing the private sector rather than releasing the private sector's great job creation potential. Similarly, the May 30, 2009 cover of *The Economist* reads: "Business in America: Its Next Problem – Big Government." The report begins with a full-

JOB CREATION

page 1930s-era black and white photo of an unemployed person selling apples for a nickel, with the ominous headline: "Surviving the Slump". The report assails how bad the U.S. economy is, how it will stay that way for the foreseeable future, and suggests strategies to survive this depression-*esque* situation. However, it at least identifies the culprit: big government's inability to comprehend the private sector's incredible job creation potential, and its consistent reluctance to release that force.

Our intent is to lay out a very clear and logical rationale about how to foster job creation in the US economy, and this hinges on a fundamental understanding of *The Certainty Factor*. In short, as the private sector looks out to the near-, intermediate-, and long-term economic landscape, decisions about infrastructure modernization, expansion, business creation, research and development, and creating more jobs will be based upon the relative certainty of a favorable business climate, to fuel strong positive perspectives and expectations about future economic activities. Chapter One provides a basic overview of entrepreneurs, innovation, and the *invisible hand* – the three main players in private sector job creation. This crash course in American private enterprise leads into how ideas create companies, which then create jobs, and finishes with a synopsis of the U.S. economy's long-standing track record of resiliency. In Chapter Two we summarize the last 100 years of employment in the U.S., and then focus on the last decade and the current situation in 2010 – after which we introduce a detailed overview of *The Certainty Factor* and the three basic ways it functions.

With this background in place, Chapter Three explains how the private sector views job creation and the role of *The Certainty Factor* in that, while Chapter Four exposes the weaknesses and lack of substance in the government's contrary view of job creation, and how it actually disregards *The Certainty Factor*. Chapter Five then presents the clear and significant differences between wealth creation (a hallmark of the private sector) and wealth redistribution (the increasingly nonsensical hallmark of the philosophy driving government fiscal policies), and how the latter actually cripples *The Certainty Factor*. Chapter Six introduces the process and benefits of primary job creation - The *Certainty Factor* in action. Chapter Seven follows this up by explaining secondary job creation and the ripple effect that stems from initial hiring due to geometric impacts of *The Certainty Factor*. In Chapter Eight we examine some of the very best business models of American private enterprise, and show how both billion-dollar corporations and start-up entrepreneurs create new jobs based upon *The Certainty Factor*. Then in Chapter Nine, we lay out our straightforward proposal for how to jump-start meaningful and sustainable job creation in our economy, and how these relate to *The Certainty Factor*.

Chapter Ten then concludes with an empirical review of the added benefits that accrue to private sector job creation, including improved tax revenues (even with lower tax rates), additional capital and lower costs of capital, and a sustainable *Certainty Factor* resulting in *even more jobs!* Our hope is this presentation makes the case for job creation so easy to understand, even a local, state, or federal bureaucrat should be able to get it.

Author Retrospectives

The simplicity of the logic supporting entrepreneurial job creation reaches into our earliest experiences, when simple realities dictated our own enterprising actions. In the late 1960s, I (Dave) used to go down to the New Jersey Transit stop in my hometown with two friends and shine shoes for commuters waiting for their 40-minute train ride to Penn Station in midtown Manhattan. Men stood on the platform in tan trench coats, reading newspapers, and sipping coffee. We asked if they wanted a quick polish for 50¢ right on the spot, and had a 75% positive response rate. This business model was crystal clear to us, even in elementary school. A can of Kiwi® shoe-polish was $2.00 at Oppenheimer's dry goods

JOB CREATION

store across from the train station on Broadway. We knew we could get 20 shines per can, so that was 10¢ per customer cost of materials, and left us with 40¢ gross profit (80% margin per shine). The only other variable cost was our labor. There was no fixed overhead. My assets were simply a small wooden box with a block nailed on top where the commuter set his shoe, an applicator, a soft shine-brush, and one of my mom's old dishtowels for the final buffing. Private enterprise took care of creating those three jobs. New Jersey commuters with discretionary coinage in their pockets stood as a captive market waiting on a train's arrival. We came to them, they didn't have to move – just raise their shoes up 8" and set them on the block. In about four minutes, they had a nice shine, and didn't miss their train. The profit incentive was eloquently simple, and strong certainty about this market fueled positive expectations, which resulted in our economic actions. Twenty shines at 50¢ each did $10 in revenue (quarters, dimes, and nickels). Total cost of goods for those 20 shines was $2. With no overhead, that left $8 operating profit, which nicely compensated me for my labor time. One can of black polish per week, one can of brown every other week, and I made $48 a month (that's $203 in 2010 inflation-adjusted terms). Not bad for a 10-year old. And sometimes I even got a tip when a happy customer might give me a dollar bill and say "keep the change, kid".

No government directive to fund "youth enterprise." No federal spending to explore incentives for new businesses. No state budget program subsidizing local commuters to support cottage industries. No tax-funded grant to buy me a shoeshine kit and supplies. Just classic, trustworthy, individual American private enterprise at work; putting myself to work, with a crystal clear profit incentive, while accepting the risk of asking commuters if I could shine their shoes. Smith's *invisible hand* filled the gap for consumers who wished they could get their shoes shined for a reasonable price while they waited for the train, without having to leave the platform or stop reading their paper. It was a true win-win, and the market afforded the opportunity for success. Was

JOB CREATION

there competition? Of course. Did that dissuade me? No. If they wanted to sit inside the terminal on the tall leather chair, put their feet on the iron-scrolled shoe-rests, and pay $1.50 for a "professional" job from *Nick's Shine*, it was their choice. Choice always makes for a better market, layered with several options at different prices and quality, so there are product-service solutions for a wide range of customers throughout the market.

I also delivered the *TV Guide* once a week direct to 67 homes on my local route. It was 15¢ at stores and newsstands, but 40¢ from me right to your door. I paid the dispatch office downtown 10¢ an issue and kept 30¢ gross profit. That was $20 a week. After that, I moved on to the daily *News-Tribune* newspaper. A larger route with daily delivery, but larger sales and income for me. By the time I got to college, I looked for an "out" from the on-campus jobs in food service and the van-pool, and started painting kitchens, bathrooms, and garages in homes around our Westchester County campus. I would go door-to-door to get the jobs set up. I then hired friends (job creation) and other students from my school to do all the scraping, tying back the bushes, laying drop cloths, and masking windows. I paid a local contractor who had a professional airless sprayer to come in and spray the house in a day or less. When he left, the hourly-rate students came back in and we painted all the trim, removed the masking, cleaned the windows, removed all the tarps, and raked. I charged around $750 per house, paid the airless spray guy around $200, paid the hourly students around $200, and all the paint usually ended up being about $150. I usually cleared $200-$300 per house (25% to 40% margin) and got to the point where I sometimes had one kitchen, one basement, and one exterior job going at three different sites simultaneously. When I graduated college, I had over $10,000 in the bank to cover all my tuition, books, and living expenses so I could move to Boston and complete my MBA in finance full-time without having to work while in school. By August of 1982, I had my graduate degree and went to work with a downtown investment bank. My father asked me how I paid for

JOB CREATION

grad school ("where'd you ever get that kind of money?"). It was very satisfying to simply smile, pat him on the back, and tell him not to worry about it, that I simply "figured it out on my own."

In very similar manner, I (Andy) grew up in suburban Ohio - an area that was in the process of changing from farms and agriculture to a suburb for people working in Cleveland who no longer wanted to live in the city. We had a small ranch house across the street from the farmhouse that originally dominated our street. There were about eight other houses in our neighborhood. Each of these houses was on a three to five acre lot with at least an acre of lawn. In 1960, when I was 10 years old, my father bought a Bolens® tractor to cut the acre or so of lawn that surrounded our house. Once I learned how to use the tractor, he offered to let me use it to cut other lawns in the neighborhood as long as I would cut our lawn once a week and pay for the gas and oil to operate the tractor. I went around to the neighbors and offered to cut their lawns for $5. I had one neighbor who agreed that I would cut his lawn each week and three others who said they would use me as needed. The elements of this enterprise were simple. I wanted to make a profit. To cover the costs of rent for the equipment, all I needed was my time once a week and the gas and oil necessary to mow our lawn. Gas and oil were cheap and I easily covered the costs to operate the tractor with the one assured job per week. In fact, I spent about $2 per week on gas and oil and made $5 per week leaving me a hefty $3 profit. Since the equipment costs were fixed, the more lawns I mowed, the more money I made. As such, I made sure I did a very good job on our lawn and my once-a-week lawn with the intent to instill confidence in my neighbors that I could do the job well. By the end of that summer, I had two more assured customers and two others who used my services regularly. I grossed $20 a week with expenses of $5. For the next few years, I made $60 a month during the summer and felt pretty proud of myself. That kind of pride is not something you get from your parents giving you money or, later in life, from the government doing so.

JOB CREATION

During the summer of my first year in college, jobs were hard to find. With my father's help, I painted our house that June and thought we had done a good job. I went out and bought a couple of hanging scaffolds, some paint brushes, an aluminum ladder, borrowed my dad's extension ladder and step ladder, and ran a small ad in the *Chagrin Valley Times* offering to paint houses for a very reasonable price. I had an old Ford Econoline® van with a rack on top, so I was in business. The hard part was estimating how much to charge. One or two underestimates solved that problem and gave me the necessary education. I would charge them a set amount plus the cost of the paint. I started out painting houses with a friend. Eventually I hired three of my friends to paint with me and gave them half of what we got paid for the job. I kept half for myself because I owned the equipment, ran the ads, and got the jobs. By the end of that summer I had saved $4,000. By the end of the next summer, I saved an additional $5,000. I never had a loan for college and my parents never paid for any of my education. Again, the pride and satisfaction you feel from putting yourself through college is different than what you feel about an education paid for by your parents or the government. I also employed some friends who would otherwise have spent their summers engaging in less lucrative pastimes.

These early personal experiences were logical opportunities and made complete sense for someone willing to take on some risk, be creative, and work hard. They naturally resulted in private sector job creation, and were a direct function of *The Certainty Factor.* Our hope is that these anecdotes and our following ten chapters will resonate strongly with our readers. Job creation is so incredibly basic and common sense as an endeavor. Government's primary role should be to get out of the way and let individuals be enterprising, creative, innovative, and hardworking. Government should remove barriers, constraints, and other hindrances that discourage individuals from pursuing innovative enterprise. Job creation is a natural result of *The Certainty Factor* and pursuing

JOB CREATION

market opportunities. Over time these translate into increased demand, more competition, improved quality, lower prices, higher profits, and more income for workers. There will always be inherent risks in the free market. Yet, if successful, the enterprise benefits its employees and all market distribution channels. When the business scales, it will require more workers for production, sales, customer service, and internal operations. Multiply this growth on numerous levels across dozens, hundreds, and thousands of market spaces, and the overall economy expands and business value (wealth) increases.

People have jobs, and choices of jobs, and income from those jobs to spend on goods and services throughout the economy. This is a process the government is neither qualified nor equipped to control or direct. But far too many politicians believe that government can orchestrate economic activity through regulations and taxation. We beg to differ. This book offers a straightforward analysis of job creation, and how it really works, and why government doesn't understand it. We trust our readers will easily and immediately recognize the logic and common sense of private sector, free market job creation, and the word will get out on a national level to politicians and professional bureaucrats at every level, to change their fundamental thinking, so as to pursue policies that promote enterprise, creativity, innovation, research and development, and sustainable job creation. There is still time to change our current course, to reduce government's role in centralized planning, stop stimulus spending, cut existing taxes, halt any new taxes, release the entrepreneurial energy inherent in the free enterprise system, and then enjoy watching the resilient U.S. economy flourish once again.

- Dave Newton and Andy Puzder
Santa Barbara, California

Chapter 1

Entrepreneurs, Innovation, and the Invisible Hand in the US Economy

> *"The confident and venturesome assume the risk,
> or insure the doubtful and timid,
> by guaranteeing to the latter a fixed income,
> in exchange for an assignment of the actual results."*
>
> — Frank Knight
> *Risk, Uncertainty,
> and Profit* (1921)

Ninety years ago, University of Chicago professor Dr. Knight captured the true core value and clarity of American private enterprise and job creation. Without specifically mentioning the *entrepreneur*, this timeless quote rightly observes that individuals who are confident and inherently venturesome are the ones who step up and heartily take on the risk of engaging in enterprise development. This is the heart and soul of the U.S. economy and the only true basis for job creation. Start-up ventures, multibillion-dollar corporations, and every form and size of business in between, have consistently created jobs based upon their outlook about what the future economic climate is likely to be for selling their products and services in the market. A major part of "assuming the risk" involves figuring out how the various facets of the competitive and regulatory landscape will directly impact the success of the venture. If the risks are manageable, the venture moves forward. If the risks are unmanageable, the venture either folds up, or goes into a tentative holding pattern

JOB CREATION

until the risks can be reduced or eliminated. And the incentive for moving forward is always those "actual results" that the venture is expected to produce. Sometimes the actual results are a loss, sometimes only breakeven. But the primary expectation of venture development is that the actual results will be profit. That's how new ideas get started; that's how innovation happens, that's how the U.S. economy works.

Innovation and new processes are what make products and services improve their features and performance over time, while decreasing production costs, and dropping prices for the end-users. Innovation and creativity bring about competition on all multiple levels. This is how new industries are born. Jobs are created as ventures launch. Jobs are created when firms grow and expand. Jobs are created as new industries are initiated from break-through innovation. Firms large and small (the "confident and venturesome") pursue all kinds of new market opportunities, and they always need new employees to get all that additional work done. That is how job creation works. It is the most natural outcome of a vibrant private sector, with free markets, and accessible capital. Wages and salaries are paid to the workers, while the owners are assigned the "actual results" of the venture's outcome. Because the ultimate outcome is unknown at inception, the American private enterprise system requires, and has always included, BOTH risk-prone creators of new businesses, and risk-averse employees who do the operations work of those very same businesses. That's what makes it work so well.

The empirical results are clear, start-up companies and other emerging ventures create the majority of lasting job growth. (Courtney Rubin, INC. ONLINE (AUGUST 13, 2010), http://www.inc.com/ news/articles/2010/08/startups-create-lasting-job-growth.html). Start-ups are primarily responsible for net new job growth in the U.S., and "the majority of the employment they generate remains as new firms age, creating a lasting [positive] impact on the economy." (Pruitt, B., "Jobs Created By Start-Up

JOB CREATION

Companies Have Long-Lasting Economic Impact", *Kauffman Foundation* – August 2, 2010) http://www.kauffman.org/newsroom/jobs-created-by-startup-companies-have-long-lasting-economic-impact.aspx). Michael Milken, in a 2009 speech to the *UCLA-Anderson Economic Forecast*, noted, "Small and mid-sized companies historically have been responsible for creating the overwhelming majority of new jobs in the private sector; one of the most-common misconceptions about our private enterprise system is that large companies, such as the Fortune 500, are integral to the process of job creation in this country; [however] the truth is quite the opposite" (Quotes by *Mike Milken*, Business, Finance and Society, http://www.mikemilken.com/quotes.taf).

Our premise is that government should step aside, get out of the way, and let the private sector function without the barriers and legislative encumbrances that limit free markets and access to capital. Here's how our U.S. economy really works, how jobs have always been created, and how it has fared over the last century.

A Crash Course in American Private Enterprise

Job creation is entirely indivisible from American private enterprise. This form of free market capitalism is an efficient system for both wealth creation and distribution. It is built on the premise that individuals are free to take business risks, be ambitious, and pursue their own ideas through creativity and innovation. They can also exercise property rights and retain the benefits (the "actual results") of their labors. American capitalism provides incentives that encourage individuals to succeed to the fullest potential of their capabilities and vision. This motivation describes the *invisible hand* that fills the gaps in meeting all kinds of product-service needs throughout our economy. Innovative ideas resonate with end-users in the market. Value is then created, and over time, markets expand with higher levels of productivity and wealth accumulation. That wealth becomes the basis for capital investments into subsequent innovation.

JOB CREATION

At the heart of this system is the entrepreneur; the individual whose creativity and ambition drive a growing economy. Entrepreneurial vision, innovation, hard work, and acceptance of risk create profitable self-sustaining businesses. Profitable self-sustaining businesses create jobs, which generate additional wealth for multiple layers of investors and employees. These jobs further distribute the wealth and, in turn, create additional tangent companies with even more jobs, as employed individuals further manage their wealth by spending or investing it. Every form of enterprise expansion, from the launch of a nascent endeavor, to the pursuit of a new joint venture among multinational conglomerates, to investments in R+D that investigate the potential for new product-service applications and opportunities, to the opening of additional facilities – these ALL create jobs . . . every time, without fail, no variation . . . in other words, this is axiomatic.

Economic systems dependent on factors other than entrepreneurial creativity and ambition historically have fared very poorly. The feudal aristocracies prevalent prior to the American Revolution generally suppressed the individual entrepreneurial spirit through regimented and class-based social structures. If a society were lucky enough to have an entrepreneur in the correct class at the correct time, it could make slow and grudging progress towards a more dynamic economy. More often, individuals in the upper classes were content to live with their inherited positions or wealth, more focused on increasing or maintaining what they had than in increasing wealth for the general population. The ruling class viewed the lower classes (the bulk of the population) as existing to serve the upper classes with very few realistic opportunities for upward mobility. Governments served to restrain entrepreneurial ambition rather than to encourage it.

JOB CREATION

Socialist economies, particularly in communist countries, have always operated in a similar manner. As everyone works for the common good, rather than in pursuit of individual benefit, there is very little motivation to innovate or take entrepreneurial risk. Why work harder or smarter than your co-workers, or take more risks, if you are unable to keep the rewards? Why increase your individual productivity if you will receive no added benefit. The limited economic benefits in such societies generally go to a ruling political class. To move into the upper echelons of power and reap the benefits of whatever wealth may exist; one must go through the political hierarchy, rather than the economic structure. As such, those wishing to improve their economic circumstances seek political power rather than initiating ventures that contribute to economic prosperity. Such systems invariably result in a concentration of power in a small group of political leaders and little or no economic growth or wealth creation. The one exception has been China, which essentially modified its socialist economic policies and adopted capitalist principles to an extent no one would have anticipated in the days of Mao and his Little Red Book. The result has been an economic surge, and a growing class of financially secure individuals seeking increasingly greater levels of personal freedom.

The American experience, on the other hand, has been based since its inception on personal freedom and a federal government of limited powers. This emphasis on limited government and the potential of free individuals has encouraged entrepreneurial innovation and risk taking as individuals recognize that they retain the rewards for being first with a new idea or product and for taking the risks necessary to make it profitable. The framers of our Constitution intended the federal government's position in the economic structure as that of a facilitator of commerce and - to the extent states attempted to create inequitable advantages for themselves or their citizens through discriminatory legislation - a regulator of commerce. In essence, the framers created a federal government of limited powers that would facilitate free enterprise

JOB CREATION

and regulate attempts to make it less free. The creation of the United States Postal Service is a good example of how the framers intended the federal government to be a facilitator of free enterprise in an interdependent national economy. The Constitution's commerce clause, which empowers the federal government to regulate commerce between the states and with foreign nations, is a clear statement of the federal government's regulatory powers. The Bill of Rights went further in fostering individual entrepreneurial activity by actually creating protections for individual property rights from an over-reaching federal government. These protections included the rights essential to encouraging entrepreneurial activity, which include: a) the right not to be deprived of your property without due process of law, b) a prohibition on the government taking private property for public use without just compensation, and c) the right to a jury trial in all civil cases involving more than twenty dollars.

In the business context, the results of this structure of limited government and personal freedom have been nothing short of phenomenal. For over two hundred years, American entrepreneurs and innovators have enriched not only this nation but have served as the economic engine for much of the rest of the world. As a nation, we have witnessed more economic affluence across broader socio-economic classes than any nation in human history. The real drivers of our national economy have been and continue to be the small firms that entrepreneurs across the country create and sustain by their imaginations and hard work. These are not only our nation's primary job creators; they also foster the development of larger self-sustaining business enterprises. Virtually every large business enterprise, including McDonalds, Coca Cola, Microsoft, Apple, Ford, and Wal-Mart, started with an idea or a product under the most humble of circumstances driven by individuals unrestrained by either an oppressive class structure or pervasive government control.

JOB CREATION

The framers clearly intended that the federal government would advance the free enterprise system and thereby release the entrepreneurial potential of its citizens. The framers did not intend that the federal government would become a means to accumulate power, a focal point for the redistribution of wealth, or a retardant of economic growth. This is not to say that the framers intended, or that the Constitution supports, unrestrained or predatory business practices. For example, antitrust and securities laws are two very defensible commerce clause-based regulatory frameworks that serve to actually level the business playing field and to encourage broader and more informed entrepreneurial activity. However, it is clear that the framers were not attempting to create a pervasive government that would dominate and direct our nation's economy.

Ironically, in recent years the greatest threat to this phenomenally successful system for generating economic growth and prosperity has become the very government the framers created to facilitate free enterprise and to regulate attempts to make it less free. Beginning with the Great Depression and continuing over the past 60 years, individuals who rejected the notion of a limited government intended to facilitate and protect free enterprise have increasingly attempted to use the federal government to direct and manage our economy. This has resulted in astounding growth in the size and scope of government creating a massive bureaucracy so extensive it is almost beyond control. Increasingly, entrepreneurs are faced with a structure of regulations and taxes that impede entrepreneurial activity, discouraging investment, risk taking and job creation. Every new government program seems to need higher taxes, more bureaucracy and greater deficit spending. The resulting regulations and taxes are contrary to the very notion of free enterprise. They discourage entrepreneurial business development and growth; reducing both wealth and job creation. When government engages in such activities, it places our entire economic structure at risk based on a mistaken belief that the most effective role for government with economic growth

JOB CREATION

is to direct and manage the economy rather than to facilitate entrepreneurial activity and regulate attempts to make it less free.

The heart of the problem is that government simply fails to understand the essence of either wealth or job creation. The positive economic impact of private sector jobs reaches well beyond the jobs themselves. If successful, private sector businesses create jobs not only for their direct employees but also for a myriad of people stretching out in concentric circles from the business itself. For example, virtually any retail business such as a restaurant, hardware, clothing or grocery store will employ a certain number of people to work directly in the store serving the public. There may also be direct employees who keep financial records, order product, handle legal or human resources issues and generally keep the business moving forward from an administrative perspective. In addition, the business will need product to sell, which creates jobs outside of the business for everyone involved in the supply chain. If the business is a restaurant or a grocery store, for example, this would mean everyone from the individuals who plant the seeds and harvests the crops to the drivers who deliver such agricultural products to their final destination. The business will also require a facility from which it can operate. The construction of this facility will employ individuals such as architects and construction workers. The facility will require repairs and maintenance, which may employ individuals such as landscapers, window washers, air conditioning or heating repairmen, and people to slurry the black top in the parking lot. The business may require some form of advertising, which could involve people from an advertising agency and actors as well as people who work at newspapers, radio and TV stations. A business that succeeds at one location may choose to grow to additional locations which would necessitate additional capital expenditures for land and buildings and further this business's impact in creating both direct and concentric circle jobs. These individuals will in turn spend the monies they earn on food, clothing, housing, medical care,

JOB CREATION

educations and entertainment creating further concentric circle jobs beyond those the business itself directly created.

The key to the success of any business is the viability of its business plan. Does the company have something that people really want? Making this determination requires an entrepreneurial vision and a desire to risk assets and a great deal of future time on that vision. If it succeeds, the benefits can be huge, not only for the entrepreneur, but for everyone the business reaches. This is the American economy's *invisible hand* of entrepreneurial vision and ambition that creates both wealth and jobs. It is the fuel that drives our economic engine. When an entrepreneur creates a private sector business, (small or large), it is also a self-sustaining venture. While the business will need customers to maintain its financial integrity and may require capital (personal investment and/or debt financing), if the free enterprise system functions properly, it will not require tax dollars to survive. Rather, private firms generate profits that actually produce personal and business tax dollars that in turn make government itself possible. To succeed, a private sector business must be self-sustaining. If it is not, it will no longer exist.

Government simply does not work this way, nor are those in government motivated to think this way. These tax-funded positions and programs operate outside the constraints of success or failure and, therefore, lack even the most basic forms of incentives such as those a private sector firm needs to succeed. Without "success" as an incentive, and being dependent on tax revenues for survival, there is only an inherent motivation for those involved in government jobs or projects to seek increases in taxes and larger government power, rather than private sector job creation and economic growth. People who enter government service generally do so out of a desire to serve, or because they are risk averse and such positions appear to be relatively secure. There are also those who pursue positions in government as a means to gain influence or power. In either case, there is no

JOB CREATION

incentive in government service to create new business ventures or to take entrepreneurial risks, because government positions are neither self-sustaining nor profit producing. In fact, government jobs are entirely dependent upon the tax revenues that individuals and self-sustaining private sector jobs produce. As such, the dollars available to pay government employees and to fund government projects should never exceed the amount of tax revenues available to pay for those jobs, as government produces comparatively little income other than through taxes. While private sector employees are tax producers, government employees are tax consumers.

Government created jobs outside of the government itself, such as those created by building roads or bridges, are similarly tax consuming rather than self-sustaining. When the road or bridge is complete, the job is over and the resulting road or bridge produces no ongoing income (unless there is a toll). Rather, they serve to facilitate commerce by, for example, making it easier to transport goods or deliver services. However, for these benefits to be meaningful, people must have incomes out of which they can purchase goods, jobs they need to get to, and cars and gas to get there. In other words, they need private sector jobs. The American capitalist system's goal is to generate economic success and spread it across a broad range of individuals. In this sense, no system has ever been more successful. Given the vastly different motives of those in government and entrepreneurs in the private sector, it is simply unreasonable to expect that increased government involvement in our economy will encourage or result in meaningful or sustained economic growth or long-term job creation. To foster the greatest economic growth and distribute it among the greatest number of people, we must limit government and encourage entrepreneurial innovation and risk taking. An ever-expanding government that directs and dominates our economy is antithetical to continued economic success.

JOB CREATION

Ideas Create Companies That Create Jobs

So how exactly are new jobs created? There are economists from every school of thought who either view the process as fairly straightforward, or a highly complex interaction of multiple variables and underlying factors, or something in between. Many of these economists always include federal, state, and local governments into the mix, as if jobs can only be initiated with some form of legislated program to make them happen. It is our contention that the creation of jobs is perhaps one of the most basic decisions implemented throughout the American private enterprise system. At its core level, it works very simply like this. A venture is aimed at meeting a specific need in a targeted market, and to accomplish that task, the entrepreneur can either do all that work, or hire others to do it. The entrepreneurs base the decision on a very simple context of resource allocation, costs, and return on that implemented action. This sequence can generate incredible internal momentum in a relatively short time period, as tasks are completed, results are measured, and additional opportunities are presented that require more workers to finish an increasingly larger and larger number of tasks.

The sustainability of the enterprise activity is a function of having a product or service that remains in sufficient demand among buyers in the targeted wholesale or retail market(s). The jobs created are then not temporary assignments or appointments for a truncated window of time, but are relatively permanent additions to the overall business model of the venture, integral to the execution of strategy as well as operational procedures. The logic usually flows something like this:

- An identifiable gap is exposed in an existing market – *"we have a problem..."*

- Creativity and ingenuity propose a way to close that gap and fix that problem

JOB CREATION

- The innovative solution is assessed for potential upside opportunities

- A forecasted trajectory is developed for how best to take action

- Financial resources are secured to pay for that action

- Individuals are recruited to perform the work

- Work gets done in line with the forecasted trajectory

- The innovative solution is introduced to the targeted users in the market

- If readily adopted, more of the solution will be demanded

- More output will be needed to supply the growing number of users

- Additional workers will be recruited to produce that increasing demand

- The original company will hire more people to do the work of added supply

- Other firms will be launched to help fill the market's similar demand

- Additional firms will introduce product-service features and price variations

- More and more jobs will be added to complete all the work to be done

JOB CREATION

This sequence is entirely organic and always dynamic across the ever-changing competitive landscape of the free market. The entire chain reaction depends very heavily on the deliberate action of one or more individuals to develop and implement a literal bridge between the conception of the innovative idea that addresses the problem-gap in the market, and how that turns into a commercially viable product or service that can be sold to targeted users. Getting all that work accomplished is how job creation happens.

The U.S. Economy's Resilient Track Record

Strong, sustained growth has been the hallmark of the U.S. economy for more than two centuries. The American private enterprise system is the greatest wealth creation and wealth distribution system ever created. Never have so many enjoyed as affluent a life style for such a sustained period of time. This is neither an accident nor a coincidence. The American private enterprise system and entrepreneurship have historically been defined by the freedom of individuals to pursue business innovation and creativity. This activity has consistently launched new companies and expanded the offerings of existing firms. These businesses have continually created new jobs across a wide range of labor and management positions.

At this point, it is important to provide a general framework for readers to readily grasp the key metrics of the historic track record for the US economy over time. One hundred years ago, the US economy (as measured by gross domestic product) produced $33 billion in goods and services. Today it has grown to $14.62 trillion, a remarkable average expansion of 6.14% per year (compounded quarterly). Think of that consistency. Through two major world wars, a decade of the Great Depression, various energy crises, and dozens of geopolitical shocks, the private sector has continued to launch new companies, create new industries,

JOB CREATION

and generate sustainable growth in both economic output and new jobs. By comparison, much has been written about China's incredible economic success and how it recently passed Japan for one quarter to become the second largest economy in the world. However, even with its phenomenal economic growth, its economy is at $4.11 trillion versus Japan's $4.61 trillion. At $14.62 trillion, even during this "Great Recession," the US economy is still over three times larger than either China's or Japan's.

Back in 1910, the U.S. population was only 92.2 million, while today it's 310 million. That's a very modest 1.2% per year growth rate (compounded quarterly). So while the population has more than tripled, the economy has grown by over 443 times! Think of it this way. That $33 billion in GDP in 1910 was spread over 92.2 million people, and averaged to just under $358 per capita. Today, that per capita amount is an astounding $47,160 – an overall economic expansion of 132 times on a per capita basis. That kind of sustainable economic growth did not come from invasive and manipulative government programs, but from hardworking Americans who pursued thousands of enterprising activities all throughout the private sector.

A survey of American firms conducted by the *National Federation of Independent Business* (NFIB) reports there are some 24 million businesses in the U.S. - 18 million (75%) sole proprietorships, and the remaining 6 million have employees. But only 18,000 of those firms have more than 500 employees, just 3,600 firms have 2,500 or more employees, and only 900 companies have at least 10,000 workers. This data is very clear. Small firms comprise a very significant proportion of the overall U.S. economy.

Given the impacts of wars, natural disasters, technology, and geopolitical changes, the U.S. economy has proven to be quite resilient in business development and consistent job creation across a wide range of industries. During the last decade, after the dot.com bubble burst, and in the wake of the 9/11 terrorist attacks

JOB CREATION

---

the following year, the U.S. economy continued to innovate and expand, with new jobs created in all sectors and industries. Table 1.1 outlines a representative sample of twenty different U.S. corporations and their continued job creation within the last ten years. Companies such as Oracle (1977), Apple (1976), Genentech (1976), and Microsoft (1975) were launched during the recessionary days of the mid-1970s, when the U.S. economy was racked by a global energy crisis and failed price controls, along with high interest rates and inflation. Just these four firms have added 135,000 new jobs to the U.S. economy since 2000. Hewlett-Packard (1939) was launched at the end of the Great Depression, while Wal-Mart (1963) and Intel (1968) started during the volatile 1960s. Wal-Mart alone has created almost one million new jobs the last ten years. Intuit (1983), Cisco (1984) and Dell (1984) launched as the 1980s microcomputer revolution was ramping up. These three firms have hired some 65,000 new workers during the past decade. Amazon (1994) and Google (1998) got started during the crazy days of the 1990s Internet explosion, and created 44,000 new jobs since their founding about 15 years ago.

These companies underscore the clear reality that American private enterprise happens in all kinds of economic and global conditions. The federal government is not, and never should try to be, a key player in the development of new firms and job creation. Market advances give rise to entrepreneurs who spot opportunities and bring new products and services to meet those needs. They create the firms that create the new jobs. The twenty companies on the prior table continue to pursue new opportunities in their markets, and no doubt, they will create additional jobs in the coming years. But the overriding negative impacts of government regulations, taxation, and deficit spending will greatly curtail the full potential of these firms' potential job creation. Entrepreneurs drive the innovation that powers the U.S. economy, as an *invisible hand* that fills gaps and meets the needs of a changing market. The track record of the U.S. economy is very strong, and its resiliency to respond to change and deal with crises

JOB CREATION

has been demonstrated time and time again. In the next chapter, we take a detailed look at the last 100 years of U.S. employment, and introduce the specific components of the *Certainty Factor* as the primary catalyst for private sector job creation.

Table 1.1

FIRM	2010 Employees	2000 Employees	Growth
Wal-Mart	2.1 million	1.14 million	+ 84%
Apple	36,800	11,728	+ 214%
IBM	399,409	343,600	+ 16%
Oracle	105,000	56,133	+ 87%
eBay	16,200 Worldwide		
	516,000 Fixed-price storefronts		
Cisco	65,550	34,00	+ 93%
Microsoft	93,000	39,10	+ 138%
Amazon	24,300	7,60	+ 220%
Hewlett-Packard	304,000	84,40	+ 260
Toyota USA	35,671	30,775 (2003)	+ 16%
Dell	65,200	34,300	+ 90%
Harley Davidson	7,900	6,700	+ 18%
Proctor + Gamble	127,000	110,000	+ 16%
AT+T	281,000	204,530	+ 38%
Genentech	6,370	4,459	+ 43%
Costco	142,000	78,000	+ 82%
Google	19,786	3,021 (2005)	+ 560%
Intel	79,800	70,200	+ 14%
Intuit	7,800	6,000	+ 30%
Pfizer	116,500	50,900	+ 129%

Source: Securities and Exchange Commission filings (www.SEC.gov)
Compiled + arranged by David Newton © 2010.

JOB CREATION

Chapter 2

100 Years of US Employment: 1910-2010

"Over the years, the U.S. economy has shown a remarkable ability to absorb shocks of all kinds, to recover, and to continue to grow. Flexible and efficient markets for labor and capital, an entrepreneurial tradition, and a general willingness to tolerate and even embrace technological and economic change, all contribute to this resiliency."

- Ben Bernanke
Chairman,
Federal Reserve

Chairman Bernanke could not have stated it more eloquently. What makes the U.S. economy so resolute is its inherent functional relationship to deal with change and innovation. Sometimes change introduces troubles, economic difficulties, and negative effects on commerce and personal income. Such shocks come out of nowhere and catch individuals, firms, and governments by surprise. There are usually a series of responses that seek to correct the immediate negative effects, while addressing the steps necessary for avoiding a similar problem again in the future. Other times change is the catalyst for fixing problems and initiating forward movement. Innovation shows itself perpetually throughout all components of the U.S. economy, as new ideas, processes, and products improve quality and efficiency while usually reducing costs and waste. In the wake of negative news,

JOB CREATION

companies re-think strategies and consumers re-adjust their spending and preferences. Recovery happens when confidence is restored in the prospects for the future. Such optimism re-ignites investment opportunities and risks are again deemed worthy of capital expenditure – be it for new assets, product innovations, or research and development. Our capital and labor markets make the appropriate adjustments for supply and demand, while pricing volatility stabilizes as uncertainty is reduced. Entrepreneurs keep thinking up great new ideas for how to close the gaps in product and service markets. Consumers, wholesale buyers, and industrial users recognize and embrace the benefits of innovation, and change the way they build, buy, produce, save, and invest – incorporating new thinking, processes, and structures into how commerce gets done.

A Crash Course in American Employment

The U.S. economy has created several hundred million new jobs over the last 100 years. Our markets are robust, they adapt readily to change and innovation, they afford individuals countless opportunities to take risks and try new things. Entrepreneurs launch new ventures; they create new products and services; they introduce competition to improve quality, reduce costs, and lower prices while improving quality and functional features. Our economy has maintained these processes while fine-tuning the art of enterprise development. This leads to new employment opportunities for millions of workers across dozens of industries across all sectors of the economic landscape.

The next task is to present a clear and concise overview of employment basics, and understand the trends of the last 100 years. The key measures include: a) the size of the US economy, as measured by the Gross Domestic Product (GDP); b) the US population; c) the number of workers employed as a percentage of the total available workforce – referred to here as the *US employment rate;* d) total spending by the federal government; and

JOB CREATION

finally, e) government spending as a percentage of US domestic economic output. For example, one hundred years ago in 1910, the US economy was just over $33 billion, with a population of around 92 million people, 94% were employed (U.S. Department of Labor), and federal government spending was $840 million (just 2.5% compared to GDP). The year 1910 serves as the 100-year baseline for understanding the track record of today's U.S. economy and employment.

Table 2.1 shows these same four measures at each decade benchmark, through the most recent data available for fiscal year 2009, and the first half of 2010. Special inserts review the end of WWII and the 1948 first post-war presidential election. After WWI and at the start of the "Roaring Twenties", the economy had grown 165% to over $88 billion, employment was generally steady at 94.8%, but federal government spending had grown 8-fold to $6.8 billion, 7.6% or triple the rate from ten years earlier. By 1928, employment had increased slightly to 95.2%. So, on average, around 19 of every 20 workers were employed for the 20 years between 1910 and 1930. At the start of the Great Depression in 1930 – the economy was only a total of three percentage points larger than it had been ten years prior in 1920. However, better than 9 out of every 10 in the workforce were employed (91.3%), while federal spending had been reduced by more than $3 billion (down 42%) to only about 4% of U.S. GDP.

Two years later, as the depression worsened, employment dropped to 76.4% in 1932, then remained relatively low at 78.3% by 1934, and was showing some slight improvement to 83.1% by 1936. Even during the worst of economic times, around 3 out of every 4 workers was employed, and that improved to over 4 out of 5 as the depression eased, heading into the second half of that decade. In 1940, before the U.S. entered WWII, employment had improved to 85.3%. Think about that – even before millions were mobilized into the war effort – a full 17 of every 20 workers were employed. The economy was 11% larger than ten years earlier in

JOB CREATION

1930, but government spending had increased 150% in those ten years, and the federal budget was now 10% of annual GDP.

Table 2.1
The US Economy + Employment: 1910-2010

Year		GDP	Employment	Federal Spending	Spending % of GDP
1910		$33.4 Billion	94.1%	$840 Million	2.5%
1920		$88.4 B	94.8%	$6.78 Billion	7.6%
1930		$91.2 B	91.3%	$ 3.96 B	4.3%
1940		$101.4 B	85.3%	$10.06 B	10%
	1945	*$223.3 B*	*98.1%*	*$106.9 B*	*47%*
	1948	*$269.1 B*	*96.3%*	*$ 35.6 B*	*13%*
1950		$293.7 B	94.3%	$ 44.8 B	15%
1960		$526.4 B	94.5%	$ 97.3 B	18%
1970		$1.038 Trillion	95.1%	$195 B	19%
1980		$2.789 T	91.3%	$591 B	21%
1990		$5.801 T	92.4%	$1.25 T	22%
2000		$9.952 T	96.2%	$1.79 T	18%
2010[1]		$14.62 T	89.6%	$3.72 T	25%

Sources: USGovernmentSpending.com;
US Dept. of Labor; Bureau of Labor Statistics.
Compiled and formatted by: David Newton © 2010

Then, just two years later, after the U.S. entered WWII, the 1942 employment rate jumped back up to 95.3% (better than 19 out of every 20 were working), and this topped out at 98.8% in 1944. Employment remained in the 95% range through the remainder of

JOB CREATION

the decade. By the end of the war, GDP had more than doubled in just six years (1940-1945) to over $223 billion. Government spending had ballooned to about half of annual GDP, with 87% of that defense-related ($93.7 billion out of $106.9 billion total).

In the post-WWII election year of 1948, the Truman Administration presided over the reduction of government spending by more than two-thirds - down to just 13% of GDP. During Truman's eight years as president, total civilian employment grew from 41.8 million working to 50.8 million – a net gain of 8.4 million new jobs, a 20% increase. (*Bush on Jobs: The Worst Track Record on Record*, WALL ST. J., Jan. 9, 2009, http://blogs.wsj.com/ economics/2009/01/09/bush-on-jobs-the-worst-track-record-on-record/). This strong job performance is generally attributed not to any of his domestic economic plans, as he opposed Republican tax cuts that helped the wartime economy transition to a commercial emphasis. Nearly all of the one-fifth increase in new jobs was a result of the huge inflow of soldiers into the civilian workforce between 1945 and 1950.

During the Eisenhower years of 1953-1961, employment ranged between a high of 97% (again, better than 19 of every 20 had a job) in 1952, and a low of 93.2% by 1958 (still better than 18 out of every 20). These years saw the rise in non-military technology jobs, as significant innovations in computers and various automated machinery created a whole new sector of the US economy. GDP was up by 50% to over $437 billion by Ike's second term election in 1956, and employment remained robust at better than 95% - again, 19 out of 20 workers had jobs. Total job creation during his eight years was 3.5 million new positions (from 50.2 million to 53.7 million), up seven percent (*Bush on Jobs*, WALL ST. J., Jan. 2009). This occurred during the "baby boom", when the U.S. population grew by some 23 million (up 13%). Eisenhower is generally criticized for keeping in place the high individual and corporate tax rates from the Korean War era, and that job growth would have been much higher had he reduced

JOB CREATION

taxes, as he presided over the first wave technology revolution of the 1950s that included major expansion of advances in television, aerospace, computers, and automotive products and services.

As John F. Kennedy campaigned during 1960, employment was 94.5%, and federal spending continued to grow, representing 18% of GDP (compared to just 15% in 1950, and only 10% in 1940). During his nearly three years in office, 3.6 million new jobs were created (from 53.7 million to 57.3 million). This seven percent increase was the same growth rate in just under three years that Eisenhower had presided over in eight years. (*Bush on Jobs,* Wall Street Journal, January-2009). Much of it is attributed to Kennedy's expressed commitment to overhaul the U.S. tax system while also reducing income taxes for both individuals and businesses. While his plan was not implemented prior to his death, the general business climate remained very bullish about the president's commitment to reduce federal spending, cut taxes, and pursue his decade-long aerospace-technology agenda to put an American on the moon.

By mid-decade, Lyndon Johnson had launched his "Great Society" initiatives, as federal spending was $118 billion in 1965, $134 billion in 1966, and $157 billion by 1967 – representing 19% of U.S. GDP. Some 11.9 million new jobs were created between 1963 and1968, as total employment went from 57.3 million to 69.2 million. (*Bush on Jobs,* WALL ST. J., Jan. 2009). This 20% increase (the same as during the Truman years) is attributed to a combination of the huge deficit spending Johnson put in place to pay for newly created programs (public service jobs) such as Medicare, Higher Education Act, the NEA, the Department of Transportation, and the multiple agencies to undertake his war on poverty. The second wave of technology jobs coincided with the last five years of the race to the moon (1965-1969), where the private sector partnered with the government to create over half the 11.9 million new jobs in the burgeoning fields of computers, aerospace, composite materials, and electronic banking. By the

JOB CREATION

election year of 1968, U.S. employment had improved to 96.2% such that, during the decade of the 1960s, there were on average 18 or 19 people working for every twenty in the U.S. labor pool.

By 1970, the US economy had for the first time in history topped $1 trillion ($1.038T), a nearly 100% expansion (97.3%) in the ten years since 1960. During Nixon's second term, US employment dropped to 94.6% (1972) and then dropped to as low as 92.3% at the close of the Ford administration (1976). Job creation was very robust as the third wave of computer growth happened during the eight years of the Nixon-Ford Administrations (1969-1976), with 11.2 million new jobs added (+16%) (*Bush on Jobs,* WALL ST. J., Jan. 2009). While Nixon hedged on tax cuts, President Ford introduced $16 billion in tax cuts that had an immediate positive impact on the economy in 1975-1976. Much of the job expansion of the Nixon-Ford years came about because of the advent of Silicon Valley's huge growth in computer hardware and software technologies, fueled not by government spending plans, but by the largest proportionate investment of venture capital into private sector new businesses in U.S. history.

Total employment remained around 93% during the Carter years (1977-1981), when 10.5 million new jobs were created during the advent of the personal computing revolution. It is widely agreed that job growth could have been much stronger had Carter not put in place various price controls, higher taxes, and failed energy policies that actually kept inflation and interest rates at record high levels. By 1981-1982 employment had bottomed out at the start of Reagan presidency at 90.3% as the U.S. economy was in recession and reeling from the residual effects of continued high inflation and interest rates. Yet, even then, after an arguable six-year recession, better than 9 of every 10 workers were still employed, and it was about to get better very quickly. By the end of Reagan's first term in 1984, 92.5% were employed, and that climbed to 94.5% at the end of his eight years in the White House. More than 16 million new jobs (+18%) were created during 1981-

JOB CREATION

1988 (*Bush on Jobs,* WALL ST. J., Jan. 2009) due to a strong combination of tax cuts, investment tax credits, accelerated depreciation schedules, and the explosion of the personal computing era. This era of unprecedented micro-computing growth, referred to as the microcosm (G. GILDER, MICROCOSM: THE QUANTUM REVOLUTION IN ECONOMICS AND TECHNOLOGY (Touchstone Press 1989)), brought personal computing and software proliferation into the office and the home, and transformed how business, education, and entertainment function. Once again, the U.S. economy's resiliency was clearly evident when 19 out of every 20 workers were employed by the close of the Reagan years.

By 1990, George H. W. Bush was now presiding over the results from the era of George Gilder's *Microcosm* - vast economic gains derived from the introduction and expansion of commercial microcomputer applications. The U.S. economy now boasted $5.8 trillion in GDP, up an incredible 108% in ten years - more than doubling in the decade from 1980 to 1990. Just over 2.5 million new jobs were created during Bush's one term, with 80% of that coming in the first two years (1989-1990), but this was just a 2.3% increase overall, on the heels of Reagan's eight years of record job growth (*Bush on Jobs,* WALL ST. J., Jan. 2009). Amazingly, all that economic expansion provided millions of new jobs in dozens of technology-related industries, and total employment remained at better than 94% heading into the 1990s, even though there was a slight economic slow-down during, and in the aftermath, of the Gulf War that expelled Saddam Hussein from Kuwait. Overall employment dropped to 92.5% as the Bush-41 term ended, linked to a short-lived economic downturn (many dubbed this a "mini-recession" from late 1991 up until the election in November 1992). Fueled by the advent of the Internet, the worldwide web, and nascent ecommerce innovations, employment quickly improved to 94% by the time of the 1994 Contract With America, and was up to just over 96% (essentially *full employment* in economic terms) as the second Clinton term concluded in 2000 alongside the burgeoning dot.com era. The internet boom created

JOB CREATION

more than 22 million new jobs and unprecedented additional tax revenues flowed into the U.S. Treasury between 1996 and 2000, resulting in a budget surplus, even as the Clinton Administration was actually increasing taxes and government spending.

In the election year of 2000, the NASDAQ peaked in March at 5,034 while the Dow Jones Industrials hit 11,722 on January 14th; GDP was up a strong 71% total during the entire decade of the 1990s, to nearly $10 trillion. Huge windfalls to federal government receipts from unexpected gains in personal income taxes, corporate income taxes, and capital gains taxes - plus the effects of the public's demand for less government spending - had reduced Washington's budget back to around 18% of GDP. As George W. Bush took office in January 2001, employment was generally holding steady, and by year-end it had dropped only a small margin to 95.3%, primarily due to the political-economic shock during the entire fourth quarter, post-9/11. It's remarkable that on the heels of the terrorist attacks on the U.S. Homeland, the economy grew to $10.6 trillion (up 6% over 2000), and by the 2004 election, 3 years into the overthrow of the Taliban in Afghanistan, and 18 months into the on-going liberation of Operation Iraqi Freedom, US employment remained at 94.5% while the economy continued to expand to $11.87 trillion (up another 12% in the two years since 2002).

Once again the U.S. economy proved to be quite resilient, with more than 19 out of every 20 American workers employed. The second term of the Bush administration had employment between a low of 94.2% (as the 2008 recession emerged) and a high of 95.4% (both 2006 and 2007), and federal spending stayed in the range of 18% to 19% of GDP. In Table 2.2 it is especially worth noting that even in the crucial aftermath of 9/11, the economy still grew consistently from 2001-2008 (much of that expansion was due to the impact of the Bush tax cuts on the consumer sector).

JOB CREATION

Table 2.2

Year	U.S. GDP	Change (year-to-year)
2001	$10.29 T	+ 2.75%
2002	$10.64 T	+ 3.40%
2003	$11.14 T	+ 4.69%
2004	$11.87 T	+ 6.55%
2005	$12.64 T	+ 6.48%
2006	$13.41 T	+ 6.09%
2007	$14.11 T	+ 5.22%
2008	$14.44 T	+ 2.33%

Source: U.S. Dept. of Commerce, BEA – www.Data360.org
Table compiled and arranged by David Newton © 2010.

During the same eight years of the Bush Administration, the stock market also continued to create new wealth as the Dow Jones Industrial Average fell to just over 8,200 right after 9/11, but then topped 14,100 just six years later in early October 2007 – up almost 6,000 points or +72%. The sub-prime lending crisis started to show its full impact heading into Q4 2008 and the presidential election, as GDP would be flat compared to Q4 2007. The economy was formally recognized as being in recession when Q1 2009 (down 1.18%) and Q2 2009 (down 2/10ths of one percent) had consecutive decreases in GDP, while employment dropped sharply to less than 90% due to the uncertainty of federal bail-outs, increased federal regulations, higher taxes, and massive new federal spending plans.

The evidence is overwhelmingly convincing. The US capitalist economy, with its free markets and robust private sector have continued to successfully advance innovation and enterprise for nearly 100 years, and have clearly demonstrated proficiency for creating jobs and maintaining generally strong employment. There was one anomaly in the 1930s' Great Depression, and a few

JOB CREATION

periods of recession, but employment over the last 100 years has generally averaged around 18-to-19 people with jobs for every twenty in the workforce. And this has been sustained even as GDP was expanding from $33 billion in 1910, to over $14 trillion in early 2010, producing a 100-year sustained average annual growth in the U.S. economy of 6.14% (compounded quarterly).

Focus on the Last Decade

The period 2000 to 2010 has been a very volatile window of time on the geopolitical front. The decade began with the collapse of the speculative dot.com bubble across the US equity markets, as the NASDAQ (5,047 on March 4th) and the DJIA (11,723 on January 14th) hit their historic to-date highs during the first quarter. The stock markets continued their slides into the fourth quarter during a hotly contested November presidential election, as the NASDAQ lost 1,631 points to 3,416 (off 32.3%) and the DJIA was down 906 to 10,817 (off 7.73%). However, employment remained very strong through year-end, with what had become a very typical average of around 19 of 20 individuals employed in the US workforce, and federal spending at around 18% of GDP. On the next page, Table 2.3 summarizes the last decade's track record for the economy and employment.

In January 2001, Bush-43 took office, and then the terrorist attacks of 9/11 occurred eight months into his presidency. The equity markets and the overall economy and employment situation could have experienced a catastrophic negative impact, but notice that GDP was up 3.4%, employment was at 95.3% for 2001 (even with the four months post-9/11), and the economy remained in steady growth of nearly 3.5% during 2002, with only a 1.1 percentage point drop in total U.S. employment.

JOB CREATION

Table 2.3
The Recent Decade: The U.S. Economy + Employment

Year	GDP	Employment	Federal Spending	Spending % of GDP
2000	$9.952 T	96.2%	$1.79 T	18%
2001	$10.29 T	95.3%	$1.86 T	18%
2002	$10.64 T	94.2%	$2.01 T	18%
2003	$11.14 T	94.0%	$2.16 T	19%
2004	$11.87 T	94.5%	$2.29 T	19%
2005	$12.64 T	94.9%	$2.47 T	19%
2006	$13.40 T	95.4%	$2.65 T	19%
2007	$14.10 T	95.4%	$2.72 T	19%
2008	$14.44 T	94.2%	$2.98 T	20%
2009	$14.25 T	90.7%	$3.52 T	25%
2010[1]	$14.62 T	89.6%	$3.81 T	26%

Sources: USGovernmentSpending.com;
US Dept. of Labor; Bureau of Labor Statistics.
Compiled and formatted by: David Newton © 2010

In 2003, which included the launch of Operation Iraqi Freedom in March, GDP was up a robust 4.69% while employment held at 94%. In Bush's re-election year of 2004, the economy was up 6.55% and employment improved slightly to 94.5%. During Bush's second term in office, the economy continued to grow at 6.5% (2005), 6% (2006), 5.2% (2007), and 2.4% (2008) – even though the second half of 2008 included the onset of the negative effects of the subprime lending crisis and the coming recession.

Barack H. Obama took office in January 2009, and as the economy shrank by 1.3%, he introduced an 18% increase in his first budget over the prior year's levels. His $3.52 trillion spending package

JOB CREATION

jumped to exactly 25% of GDP and with a deficit of $1.4 trillion (Brian Faler & Julianna Goldman, *U.S. Deficit for 2009 Totals $1.4 Trillion, Budget Office Says,* BLOOMBERG (October 8, 2009), http://www.bloomberg.com/apps/news?pid=newsarchive&sid=aA8lChe4zUQU), or roughly 40% of the entire government budget. In addition to his regular federal budget, Obama also put in place an additional $787 billion spending package that was herald as a "stimulus" for the U.S. economy to get out of the recession. It was a humungous attempt to replicate what Japan had tried six different times over the prior 20 years, namely that the federal government would fund hundreds of temporary public works-related projects with funds borrowed through new Treasury debt. The problem is that employment dropped to 89.3% as some 1.3 million jobs were lost to the recession.

The employment landscape of the U.S. economy is a fascinating conglomeration spanning amazing breadth of applications AND highly focused depth of expertise. The *Bureau of Labor Statistics* (BLS) reported that in 2008, there were 154.3 million people employed in the civilian labor force, and that total employment had grown by 10.4 million jobs between 1998 and 2008 – up 7.4% overall (U.S. DEPT. OF LABOR, USDL-09-1503, EMPLOYMENT PROJECTIONS: 2008-2018 SUMMARY (2009)). For the current year 2010, GDP is projected to be $14.62 trillion (up 2.6%), but the president is currently planning to send Congress a $3.8 trillion budget, representing an 8% increase in regular federal spending with a projected deficit of $1.3 trillion (Jeffry Bartash, *U.S. Deficit Totals $1.29 Trillion in 2010,* FOXBUSINESS.COM (Oct. 15, 2010), www.foxbusiness.com/markets/2010/10/15/deficit-totals-trillion/).
So the combined first two years of the Obama Administration will add $2.7 trillion to the national debt. To put that in perspective, only $2 trillion total was added to the national debt during the combined preceding *eight* years (2001-2008) under President Bush (the largest deficit was $458 billion in 2008). This is separate from his plans to press through perhaps an additional $150 billion in second-round "stimulus" funding (see Chapter 4 explaining why

JOB CREATION

the first stimulus did not work). On top of this, he is also set to implement $900 billion for his federal healthcare.

By the close of 2010, employment will likely remain at only 90% as the federal government continues to redirect capital resources away from private sector asset investment and new employment, and into higher taxes and big government spending programs. Employment dropped by 4.7 million workers in 2009, the largest drop in 70 years (since 1939) when the series was started. Unlike the recessions in 1990 and 2000, employees began feeling the effect of the crisis as jobs sharply declined just 10 months into the recession (Megan Barker & Adam Hadi, *Payroll Employment in 2009: Job Losses Continue,* MONTHLY LABOR REV., March, 2010, 23-33).

Although all sizes of employers were hit by the recession, smaller businesses have had the hardest time retaining employees. Yet small firms have had both the largest net *gain* in employment and the largest net *loss* in employment during this recession. Net job gains hit a historic low during the first quarter of 2009 at the all time low of 4,517,000 (Jennifer Helfand, *All Firm Sizes Hit Hard During the Current Recession*, U.S. BUREAU OF LABOR STATISTICS (March, 2010) http://www.bls.gov/opub/ils/summary_10_02/all_firm_sizes_hit_hard.htm). Unemployment topped 10% nationally during 2009, and many people that were working were forced to take unwanted part-time roles. The number of employed persons over the age of 16 fell by 5.8 million during 2009, and with much higher unemployment, the actual labor force participation rate fell by 1% compared to 2009 (Steven F. Hipple, *Labor Market in 2009: Recession Drags On,* Monthly Labor Rev., March, 2010, at 3-22.)

With regard to job creation, today's economy tends to focus on the unemployment rate. However, unemployment may "not [be] a good measure of what is happening in the economy, [because] it's drawn from a sample too small and filled with too many assumptions; absolute job losses and retail sales give a better idea

JOB CREATION

of what's really happening in the economy" (Moira Herbst, *Unemployment: Worse Than it Looks,* BUSINESSWEEK.COM (Dec. 15, 2008), http://www.businessweek.com/bwdaily/dnflash/content/dec2008/db20081212_666543.htm). Our focus remains on the number of people employed and new jobs created (or lost). The numbers on net job losses, little new job creation, and erratic retail sales throughout 2010 continue to point toward a prolonged flat – and potentially worsening – job market. The unemployment report comes out monthly and does not take into account seasonal variations, which would suggest a year-to-year report would be more accurate. Also the unemployment rate does not necessarily assist in predicting a specific economic future, although it does confirm a wide range of economic trends (Kimberly Amadeo, *Employment Statistics History,* ABOUT.COM: US ECONOMY (Sept. 5, 2010) http://useconomy.about.com/od/economicindicators/a/Job-Stats. htm). In January 2010, U.S. unemployment was at 14.8 million people, and the western states had the largest fluctuation of unemployed persons per job opening at almost 7-to-1. (Katherine Klemmer, *Job Availability During a Recession,* U.S. BUREAU OF LABOR STATISTICS (March, 2010), http://www.bls.gov/opub/ils/summary_10_03/job_availability.htm). "A majority of states saw their unemployment rates drop by May 2010. But the widespread declines were mainly because people gave up looking for work and were no longer counted. The West region [still] remains the highest unemployment area in the United States." (Martin Crutsinger, *Unemployment Rate Drops in 37 States,* MFG. BUS. TECH. (June 22, 2010) http://www.mbtmag.com/Content.aspx?id =453).

After the dot-com boom (decline started in March 2000), Silicon Valley went through some large changes, as overall employment declined by 17%, while wages managed to increase by 36% during the same period. Only Aerospace, Pharmaceuticals, and Scientific Research had increased employment, while the Computer System Design sector had the highest employment in both 2001 and 2008. (Amar Mann & Tony Nunes, *After the Dot-Com Bubble: Silicon*

JOB CREATION

Valley High-Tech Employment and Wages in 2001-2008, BUREAU OF LABOR STATISTICS (August 2009- http://www.bls.gov/opub/regional_reports/200908_silicon_valley_ high_tech.htm).

What does this all point to in the near-term? Projected future federal deficit spending, perhaps more "stimulus" programs, and a wildcard federal healthcare plan (that no one in the private sector or Washington understands) together create huge uncertainty about interest rates, inflation, and business prospects for expansion. As such, companies are reticent to make significant financial commitments for growth and hiring new workers. New job openings were up 10.5% in the first half of 2010, as described by the Labor Department, although the hiring rate remain unchanged as employers chose not to hire during that time. (Sara Murray, *More Job Openings, but Employers Slow to Hire*, WALL STREET JOURNAL (June 8, 2010) http://blogs.wsj.com/economics/2010/06/08/more-job-openings-but-employers-slow-to-hire/).
"This was the first business cycle where a working age household ended up worse off at the end than at the beginning." (Neil Irwin, *Aughts Were a Lost Decade for U.S Economy, Workers*, WASHINGTON POST (Jan. 2, 2010) http://www.washingtonpost.com/wp-dyn/content/article/2010/01/01/AR2010010101196 .html). But there was healthy job growth in each of the previous two decades (1980-1989 during the PC revolution, and 1990-1999 during the dot.com/internet era), as America produced huge gains in new jobs throughout the private sector. (Fred Goldstein, *Mass Unemployment Is Here to Stay*, WORKERS WORLD (Feb. 28, 2010) http://www. workers.org/2010/us/unemployment_0304/).

In February 2010, the nation's unemployment rate hit 10.4%, representing about 15 million workers. Among workers 25 years and older without a high school diploma, it was 15.6%, while it was 10.5% for high school grads, but only 8% for those with an associate's degree or some college work completed (Bureau of Labor Statistics). Washington, DC as well as 16 other states recorded jobless rates greater than 10%. (Phil Izzo,

JOB CREATION

Unemployment Rates by State: Nevada Overtakes Michigan for Nation's Worst, WALL STREET JOURNAL - June 18, 2010) http://blogs.wsj.com/economics/2010/06/18/unemployment-rates-by-state-nevada-overtakes-michigan-for-nations-worst/). California currently holds the third highest unemployment rate in the United States with 12.4%, Michigan is second at 13.0%, and Nevada is the leading state with 14.4% unemployment. (*Unemployment Rates for States*, U.S. BUREAU OF LABOR STATISTICS (Oct. 22, 2010) http://www.bls .gov/web/laus/laumstrk.htm). The west coast continues to post the highest unemployment rate at 11.8% followed closely by the North East with 11.2%. North Dakota experienced the only statistically significant job increase for the year with an increase of 6,000+ new jobs. (*Regional and State Employment and Unemployment Summary*, BUREAU OF LABOR STATISTICS (October 22, 2010) http://www.bls.gov/news.release/laus.nr0.htm). Table 2.4 shows the worst long-term unemployment (mostly Eastern states) in the recent recession, the start of the dot.com era (1992), and the start of the PC revolution (1983). The top five in each were states with the highest overall taxes on individuals and the private sector.

Table 2.4
Worst Long-Term Unemployment

2009	1992	1983
Michigan	Connecticut	West Virginia
South Carolina	Massachusetts	Ohio
Georgia	Rhode Island	Pennsylvania
Rhode Island	West Virginia	Michigan
Connecticut	New Jersey	Wisconsin

Source: Economic Policy Institute –
Data from Current Population Survey.
Kevin Hall, "Record Number of Unemployment"
Socialistworker.org - June 2010

JOB CREATION

The Certainty Factor

The core underlying rationale for our book is what we term *The Certainty Factor*, and it works like this. The two groups that comprise the private sector - businesses and individuals - make decisions about investing, borrowing, and spending based primarily on their expectations, or outlook, on the future. Certainty is then linked indivisibly to *positive* prospects, and the opposite is true, that greater uncertainty is directly related to *negative* future prospects. In this context, risk is inversely related to certainty. When the future environment is projected to be *positive*, with lower taxes, steady and reasonable interest rates, low inflation, and less government regulation and intervention into private sector transactions, that translates to strong certainty about expectations, and that in turn means lower risk for engaging in investments, borrowing, and spending. On the other hand, when the future environment is projected to be *negative*, with higher taxes, volatile and higher interest rates, increased inflation, and more government regulation and invasion into private sector commerce, there is reduced certainty (more <u>un</u>certainty) about expectations, and so greater risks associated with investing, borrowing, and spending plans.

In its simplest form, an increased (positive) certainty factor means businesses and individuals are more likely to be actively engaged in new opportunities and transactions. They will invest their capital, borrow additional resources, and make purchases to modernize, upgrade, expand, and hire new workers. But a reduced (negative) certainty factor means businesses and individuals will stay on the sidelines in a risk-averse position – protecting their cash – or will postpone investments, taking on new loans, and buying goods and services, while they take more of a "wait-and-see" stance. In this latter risk-averse mindset, the private sector seeks to hedge their financial positions against the reduced certainty that translates into negative expectations.

JOB CREATION

When the certainty factor is strong, positive expectations drive new investments, new borrowing, and new spending. Increased government deficits and total debt, bigger spending programs, higher taxation, and more regulations always mean a reduced certainty factor, and negative expectations. In response to these, businesses and individuals step back from the markets and disengage from taking on new projects, and not only do they fail to create new jobs, but they also generally lay-off existing workers as a way to reduce the financial burden of their fixed overhead expenses. Decreased government deficits mean less total debt and better monetary policy. Fewer federal spending programs, lower taxes, and less regulation always mean an increased *Certainty Factor,* and positive expectations. As such, businesses and individuals have optimism to be fully engaged in their markets, taking on new projects, increasing R+D budgets, improving infrastructure and capital assets, and hiring more workers.

When senior management at a company contemplates decisions about adding new facilities, improving infrastructure, modernizing plant and equipment, putting more funds into R+D, and pursuing opportunities in new markets, each of these always includes creating new jobs. For such decisions, the potential benefits that will accrue to the firm must be examined relative to the risks associated with each action. And it's the same for individuals when they consider remodeling the house, buying a major appliance, adding a monthly payment for a new car, saving for college, or taking a vacation. When the future is more certain with positive expectations, businesses and individuals will execute such decisions. The reduced risk from a strong *Certainty Factor* improves the value of the perceived benefits. But when the future is less certain with negative expectations, those decisions are generally put on "hold" because the greater uncertainty and increased risk call into question the accrued value, and perceived benefits seem less likely. Throughout the following chapters, we will clearly define how the private sector functions based upon this *Certainty Factor.* And we will expose the backward thinking of

JOB CREATION

most government perspectives, which actually reduce - or cripple - the certainty factor, and works against job creation. In each case, the best policies and approaches to spur job creation are those that reduce (and in many cases eliminate) government involvement in the economy, thereby increasing *The Certainty Factor* and positive expectations among firms and individuals throughout the private sector. In the next chapter, we'll look at how the private sector defines job creation, and tie in the hiring decision to the *Certainty Factor.*

Chapter 3

How the Private Sector Views Job Creation

*"When new knowledge makes
old job skills obsolete,
firms want to employ workers
who already have that knowledge."*

- Lester Thurow,
Former Dean,
Sloan School at MIT

The private sector has a very different view of job creation when compared to the government's definition. In chapter one, we explained the process of how innovative ideas launch new companies, and it's those companies that then create the new jobs. In addition, existing firms also spot new opportunities in the market, pursue R+D, and look to expand their product-service offerings to wider audiences, which also create jobs. These new jobs created in the private sector are now part of the company's regular business model. The work getting done is a consistent component of the firm's output function. The wages and salaries have become line items in the budget. These workers make direct contributions to the output of goods and services that are sold in the market. There are no temporary grants, government appropriations, or artificial legislated gimmicks paying for these workers. The decision to hire new employees was made based upon the vitality of the firm, and the managers allocated company resources to pay wages for this additional work that needs to get done. These jobs help generate revenue for the firm, and as such,

JOB CREATION

the workers are then tax *contributors* to the economy. There are no special regulatory provisions required to merit this new hire. Funding for private sector job creation comes directly from the private sector, as an intentional capital investment in the business.

Workers bring a wide range of skills and experience to the job market. The plain realities of the U.S. economy demonstrate repeatedly that the infusion of new knowledge is perpetual. Job creation in the private sector follows this knowledge renewal. Sometimes it's incremental and continuous, other times its revolutionary and discontinuous. In both the near-term and long-term, innovation renders the existing paradigm of any product, service, manufacturing process, or market at best under siege, and at worst irrelevant for future applications. This describes another manifestation of the *invisible hand* functioning within free market competition. This kind of on-going systematic progress and obsolescence creates the cycles of innovation that produce continuous improvement, while at various junctures punctuate radical new designs and functions. When "old skills" are no longer viable, it's not a problem for the private sector, or time to panic as established norms are challenged. Instead, it simply signals another benchmark in the natural life of the market, as new knowledge presses further out the boundaries of what is possible.

Job creation in the private sector is therefore the result of companies needing more workers to handle plans for forecasted growth and expansion. The decision to hire is purely based on the economics of the firm. True, adding new jobs increases company expenses, but the firm agrees to take on those new payroll costs because of expected increases in sales. The labor market functions on the fundamental principle of supply and demand. A new job is not a guaranteed position for life. Its longevity is tied indivisibly to the future performance of the enterprise. Certain skilled workers provide labor efficiency gains that accrue to the firm's output function, so the firm is willing to pay for that. Job creation generally follows in lock step with all cycles of new knowledge

JOB CREATION

introductions. We've all heard the old adage of how a factory could not continue producing buggy whips if the clear direction of the market was moving away from horse-drawn carriages and over to the new automobile. So too, a service technician cannot remain focused on improving repair skills for the manual typewriter, if emerging electronic typewriters are the new models of choice. Yet, even that advancing job skill is only for a season, as desktop computing and word-processing then render even the most advanced electric typewriters obsolete. This exercise in cycled-substitutions over time is what drives job creation and labor markets in the private sector. Various accounting, finance, and production metrics form the evaluation criteria for private sector job creation, as the decision to hire is a function of trade-offs between capital and labor, the impact of supply and demand in the labor markets, and return on investment to the company.

Capital & Labor, Supply & Demand, ROI

The private sector views job creation as fundamentally a simple business decision. It involves several measures learned in any introductory economics class. First, the managers of the company forecast sales in the market, and put in place a plan to meet those sales, manufacturing a physical product or providing a service, and this also includes a plan to stand behind those products and/or services with customer support and internal operations staff. To meet that targeted output, every company targets a sufficient number of full-time and part-time employees that are needed to accomplish the tasks associated with meeting projected sales, and the related operations and support for such. Labor and capital, are then allocated in various combinations to meet production and operations requirements. Capital includes machinery, equipment, physical plant, and related hardware technologies that are employed in certain configurations to produce the goods and/or services. The decision to utilize a certain mix of capital assets directly affects how much labor will be required. It also works in reverse, as decisions about how many workers are needed will

JOB CREATION

directly impact the level of capital assets implemented in the production-output function. The trade-off between labor and capital allocations is a management decision, based on expenses and productivity. It is dependent on things like costs to acquire, costs of operations and maintenance, and the financial and technological risks of investing now versus in the future. Management also has to decide if these assets will be operating at a highly efficient level of output, or will be underutilized if demand is lacking, or be pressed into an inefficient over-utilization beyond the intended output levels.

Essentially, there are two ends of the capital-employment spectrum. On the one end, business can be very labor-intensive, with minimal capital expenditures. At the other end, operations are highly automated with large-scale capital infrastructure and minimal numbers of employees. In between, there are countless combinations of capital and labor, depending on the type of business and the overall scale of its operations. Second, the private sector decision to hire is dependent on supply and demand for workers in the overall economy, and the firm's specific industry. Individual workers are the supply side of the equation. They package their education, experience, skills, training, and enter the job market with an "offer" price. Firms are the demand side of the model. They enumerate their employment needs, and go into the job market with a "bid" price. The difference between the employee's and the firm's wage expectations is called the "bid-ask spread", and represents how closely aligned supply and demand are for a given category of employment. If individuals and firms are both working with the exact same information about the economy, the industry, the specific product-service market, and all related macro- and micro-economic data, the bid-ask spread will be fairly small and the job market is considered efficient. In other words, all the people looking for a certain type of job are generally in line with all the firms looking to fill those certain jobs, so both sides have similar expectations about the job requirements and the associated compensation.

JOB CREATION

For example, a person with a two-year computer programming certificate and five years of software code-writing experience has similar expectations about workload and compensation as the firm looks for someone with baseline skills and some mid-range prior work experience to write code. If the SUPPLY has *thousands* of similar certificate-trained code-writers with 4-to-6 years of prior experience, but the DEMAND is only for *hundreds* of open positions at firms, then the price (compensation) for that employment will be relatively lower than if there were more open positions to fill (higher demand) and less individuals (lower supply) in the job market qualified to fill them. Salaries and wages will have to go up when demand is strong in the market compared to a relatively smaller pool of workers. Other costs include the recruiting and hiring process, initial and ongoing costs of training, and the financial and technological risks of functional capabilities, as well as the quality and precision of production output. It is interesting that right now, Chinese firms are looking to the U.S. for new employees - for highly skilled workers that fit skill sets and requisite profiles; their ability to draw upon a pool of global talent [must] be closely watched. (Stan Abrams, *China Invests in Foreign Talent*, FORBES (Apr. 27, 2010) http://blogs.forbes.com/china/2010/04/27/china-invests-in-foreign-talent/).

When a certain market, industry sector, or firm has strong, positive expectations for sustainable growth over time, those expectations signals higher demand for workers with certain qualifications. Rational individuals will weigh the costs and other related risks associated with obtaining those qualifications, and over time, the job market should see increased supply of these employees, in order to fill the gap between expected increases in labor demand and the supply of workers. If the supply of workers lags behind the growth, firms will have to pay higher (premium) compensation as they bid against other potential employers for a smaller pool of qualified workers. Conversely, when a given industry or market segment has flat or negative demand expectations for certain types of workers, individuals should move

JOB CREATION

away from supplying that kind of employment. If not, there will be far too many workers chasing too few available positions, and firms will be able to offer a lower (discount) pay-rate, as the pool of workers is disproportionately large compared to the open jobs. Overall, the job market exhibits a wide range of employment types, across various industries, part-time and full-time, hourly and salary, commissions and bonuses, barter and trade, equity options and consulting. The job market has demonstrated strong efficiency over time, as the supply of labor trends alongside expected demand. Education, experience, training, and skills go through normal business cycles as employers adjust their mix of capital and labor or as technologies and innovation change.

Third, the private sector decision to hire is a function of the company's return on investment (ROI). Each new job created uses some of the firm's resources, but each new worker contributes to increased output and higher sales, and so produces a return on those direct costs of labor. The end result of these measures is that the creation of a new job ultimately has to pay for itself from the company's sales revenue. But that's what defines a private sector job as self-sustaining. The new worker is a *revenue-generator* and also contributes to the firm's eventual profitability. There can be no doubt whatsoever about the impetus behind private sector job creation. Work needs to get done and the firm creates jobs to do that work. If there is more work than one person can do, the firm will hire another person. As certain skills are required to complete work, the firm will either find someone who is already educated, trained, and has experience in that work field, or it will educate, train, and provide experience in-house to prepare a person to do that specific work. The long-term sustainability of the job is then linked to the long-term sustainability of the product or service created and sold by the firm. If the market for that product or service is vibrant, growing, competitive, and regularly innovating and improving, the jobs that do all the work associated with the firm's position in that market have a strong degree of demand for the longer term. When a

JOB CREATION

market is nascent, and the landscape of the firms and buyers is still developing, job creation is initially more tentative. As the U.S. economy is currently running its highest unemployment level since the early 1980s recession – "with 15.3 million people out of work" at the beginning of 2010 – "job seekers still outnumber openings by more than six to one, the greatest differential since the Labor Department began tracking job openings in December 2000." (Tami Luhby, *Stimulus and jobs: What the fight's all about*, CNNMONEY.COM – January 26, 2010).

The private sector hiring decision is then derived from the type or level of investment return the enterprise can achieve on the workers employed to generate the supply of products or services. Capital assets also have associated levels of investment return to the company. As such, job creation is a direct function of ROI on human capital employed in the business. Managers would not add a worker to the production-output formula without first determining what the accrued benefit will be to the firm. The private sector understands that people need to be resourced to get work done. Expending company resources on wages, salaries, and accompanying benefits is a financial decision, plain and simple. It involves risk, and trade-offs with capital investments. Those funds allocated to hire an employee no doubt had alternative places they could have been spent. Management could have utilized some sort of automated method or process to get the work done, or the work could have been outsourced to a specialty provider. However, the best ROI is typically derived from completing work in-house.

ROI is then impacted, both positively and negatively, by the legislative and regulatory environments in which the firm operates. If local, state, and federal governments back away from imposing on companies (and individuals) overly burdensome fees, taxes, regulations, and other requirements, the calculation for ROI on hiring new workers is much easier to do, and the "returns" have a more direct impact to both the firm and workers. But when governments impose layers of laws, compliance, fees, paperwork,

JOB CREATION

and multiple (and higher) taxes, ROI on new hiring is reduced and job creation is impeded.

For example, the "return" to the company in the numerator of the ROI calculation, can be reduced by all the non-economic fees, payments, taxes, and extra compliance costs imposed on the firm. In addition, the "investment" made in employing the worker (the denominator) can then be increased by similar fees, payments, taxes, and related compliance costs that must be allocated and accounted for in order to put that employee to work. As such, the "return" numerator being reduced and the "investment" denominator being increased together drop the ROI on job creation. Companies are then forced to come up with alternative ways to get the work done that will improve the ROI on the labor factor employed. Too often, the local, state, and federal landscape is always changing with new taxes, fees, and regulations that make it difficult to forecast and plan an acceptable labor ROI. Charlie Baker, the Republican candidate for governor of Massachusetts understands what is needed in his state in order to have a vibrant work force and job creation. "We need to create a level, predictable, and competitive playing field for all business here in Massachusetts, and give companies the predictability they need to hire people here, [stay here], and expand here." (Jack Nicas, *Baker Vows to Cut Business Taxes*, BOSTON GLOBE (June 11, 2010) http://www.boston.com/news/local/ massachusetts/articles/2010/06/11/baker_vows_to_cut_business_taxes/).

So then, why is it so hard for politicians to understand how to provide a great labor environment for businesses to thrive? Local, state, and federal legislatures should do everything they can to strengthen ROI associated with hiring. This happens when the "return" in the numerator increases and/or the "investment" denominator is reduced. Not only would existing jobs stay, but new jobs would be added, and all firms (new ventures and established firms) would thrive in such an environment. The problem is clearly a philosophical one, based upon completely

JOB CREATION

opposite views of how a capitalist economy functions. "Private employers are the only people who can truly sustain job growth, and create new jobs for the future; but government regulation is reluctant to take pressure off of them, because government would lose power" (R. Epstein, *Deregulate Labor Markets*, FORBES (October 13, 2009) http://www.forbes.com/2009/10/12/labor-axelrod-efca-opinions-columnists-richard-a-epstein.html).

Marginal Productivity and Economies of Scale

Adding more workers is also based upon two other economic measures: *marginal productivity* and *economies of scale*. These have a direct impact on job creation. The decision about a private sector job is entirely a function of management's plan to meet the firm's sales projections. Things need to get done. Tasks need to be performed. Some of these require highly specialized training and/or certification. Others require more general skills, while in some cases only basic manual labor is needed. Management understands that as more workers are added, there are greater efficiencies in time and output, as multiple employees working in a well-coordinated effort can produce more output as an integrated group than simply the sum of its parts. For example, if one worker can do 100 units of output per day, some might think that adding three new workers would bring daily production up to 400 units. This assumes there are no cooperative benefits among the employees. But what if the four employees work as a team, assisting one another in the various steps of the production process, and develop new sequences and division of labor to get the work finished each day? It might be that one worker could do 100 units per day, while two employees working in cooperation with each other can do 250 units per day. Adding the third and fourth members to the team might then result in 450 and 800 units per day respectively. This teamwork and division of the labor steps increase the per worker daily productivity and create a more efficient production process. The result is greater overall

JOB CREATION

output and a lower cost per unit. The incremental increase in worker output is the marginal productivity associated with the new hire. The reduced unit cost of production is the marginal cost. Together, these reduce the average cost of the goods or services and represent *economies of scale* that accrue to the firm at larger and larger output over time. In summary, the private sector views job creation as the new regular, sustainable positions added to the firm's operations. This new employment is affected by supply and demand, the trade-off between capital and labor, and the ROI of that new job to the overall output and profitability of the firm. In addition, more workers improve marginal productivity and produce economies of scale to the firm as the per unit cost of output drops over time.

Hiring and The Certainty Factor

The private sector decision to hire new workers is a direct result of *The Certainty Factor's* affect on management's expectations about the supply and demand of the labor market, the trade-off between capital and labor utilized, ROI, and the marginal productivity and economies of scale projected to accrue to the firm. When management looks out into the near-term and longer-term of the external industry-market environment, it must assess the level of certainty about interest rate volatility, inflation, consumer confidence, taxes, government spending, and regulations. If there are strong positive signals that interest rates and inflation will be relatively low and stable, consumer confidence is improving, tax burdens on individuals and companies will be reduced, and government is reining in runaway spending, this improves *The Certainty Factor* about the future and translates into positive expectations about sales, costs, and profits. Strong, positive certainty means firms will expand, modernize, and upgrade, and hire more workers. If there are mixed signals coming from the external environment, the private sector will be more hesitant to act due to greater uncertainty in some areas concerning costs, taxes, regulations, and inflation. This results in

JOB CREATION

either postponing or scaling back any plans for expanding or upgrading facilities and infrastructure, and so too postpones or scales back any new hiring.

Finally, if there are strong negative signals due to higher taxes, greater deficit spending, volatile and higher interest rates, and more government intrusion into business and individual activities, the private sector retreats to the sidelines, waiting until the environment shows signs of improvement. In this worst case scenario, the significant reduction in certainty causes individuals and companies to eliminate altogether any new purchases, financing, or investments as prospects for sales and profits are greatly reduced, while costs and taxes are expected to increase.

When federal, state, and local governments pursue policies that add more taxes and regulations, and burden the private sector's prospects for improved cash flow, they generate increased *negative* expectations that reduce *The Certainty Factor*, and actually *hinder* new job creation. Greater uncertainty also encourages firms to cut existing payrolls, which results in higher unemployment. Less federal programs, reduced deficit spending, lower taxes, and cutting back on regulations improve *The Certainty Factor*. This provides risk reduction and positive incentives to execute private sector hiring plans in support of expansion, modernization, and other growth-related strategies. A strong, positive *Certainty Factor* is also a great motivator for entrepreneurs to launch new companies, and of course hire workers. "Private businesses are the nation's critical engine for growth, innovation and job creation, yet they are being starved for credit and slammed with more taxes, government directives, and litigation exposure; this spells weaker profits and *fewer* jobs, risking a fundamental deterioration in America's private sector." (D. Malpass, *Shakedown*, FORBES (June 28, 2010) http://www.forbes.com/forbes/2010/0628/opinions-david-malpass-current-events-shakedown .html). "It is important for new small [firms] to succeed because they have high job creation rates and will help

JOB CREATION

pull [the economy] out of recession." (T. F. Cooley, *Where Are the Next Jobs Coming From?*, FORBES (February 20, 2010) http://www.forbes.com/2010/02/09/employment-entrepreneurs-jobless-recovery-opinions-columnists-thomas-f-cooley.html).

The private sector's view of job creation is based on positive expectations for strong future opportunities. These jobs are part of the business model for the company's planned production output of goods manufactured and/or services provided. These are invariably tied to upbeat forecasts for sustainable sales growth and profits. Increased positive certainty about the near-term and beyond constitutes all the incentive the private sector needs to actively pursue innovation, operational and strategic expansion, and a wide range of new market opportunities. In the next chapter, we'll review how the government defines job creation, how it is completely contrary to the private sector's perspective on the *Certainty Factor,* and why its underlying rationales actually decrease optimism and certainty, and lead to job reductions and higher unemployment.

Chapter 4

How the Government Views Job Creation

"One of the great mistakes is to judge government policies and programs by their intentions rather than their results."

- Milton Friedman

Friedman rightly recognized that hopeful intentions on the part of politicians can never be equated with positive tangible outcomes. No matter how the Beltway insiders - or our state's Sacramento politicians - continue to dream on about enacting good things for the national and state economy, the overwhelming track-record of what actually transpires after implementation of their policies remains tragic at best. This failed logic is notably captured in the ubiquitous orange signs that are displayed everywhere here in California since the *American Recovery and Reinvestment Act* (ARRA) was enacted in 2008. A pathetic stick figure of a person is lifting a shovel above what appears to be a pile of dirt, and written above this hopeful icon is the propaganda: "Putting America To Work". Entire classes of economics students should take field trips to such government signage, and there engage in the multiple levels of connotation and intonation that are both explicit and implicit in the underlying philosophical rationale for such a message. This provides the sad context for how government views job creation, and why it is so different from our prior chapter that explained how the private sector defines job creation.

JOB CREATION

This distorted worldview circumvents the plain and simple truths of introductory macro- and microeconomics. The vast majority of politicians have never run a company or managed revenues and costs to produce a profit - let alone even worked for a business. They have never been responsible for economic results such as sales revenue, costs, or profits. They don't have any understanding of capital and labor inputs, risk, and market forces. They actually believe they can envision and implement their planned egalitarian distribution of jobs, apportioned across industries and markets in a regimented fashion based upon what seems proportionate and "right" to them in their elementary (and elitist) worldview of how things *should* be. However, that is entirely contrary to sound economic principles.

In the previous chapter, we explained how managers hire new workers based upon positive expectations for the future, derived from strong *Certainty* of a favorable and stable market environment. Politicians do not understand that entrepreneurs and existing firms are the ones who spot new opportunities in the market, pursue R+D, and look to expand their product-service offerings to wider audiences. This natural incentive to increase sales and profits is the great incentive for the private sector to create jobs. But government tends to have a very negative attitude about profits. For decades, it has come up with arbitrary dollar amounts as to what constitutes a "fair" profit. Their derogatory perspective on profitability injects accusations of greed toward those in the private sector that are building wealth over time. The current administration has arbitrarily decided that $250,000 in annual compensation is the new measure by which individuals are defined as "wealthy" and have "made enough". Any earnings beyond that constitutes excess.

Central Plans: Nothing Created, No Benefits Accrued

Picture this stark image, right out of a dark, chilling, Soviet-era propaganda film. Politicians wax seemingly eloquently about their

JOB CREATION

centrally planned remedy for the national economy - a supposedly carefully calculated and measured government program that will decide *how many* new jobs will be created, and in *what industries* the new jobs should be promoted. The only problem is the setting for this policy advance is Capitol Hill in Washington, D.C., and the message is coming from our elected officials who swore an oath to "support and defend the Constitution of the United States". Many politicians continue to display two key flaws in their thinking about the economy and the role of the private sector. First, they embrace an egalitarian (socialist) philosophy that wages, salaries, sales, and profits should all somehow be level across the entire spectrum of the market. Second, they truly believe that private enterprise is a destructive zero-sum game, such that a firm experiencing success must be doing so at the expense and peril of another company. Regarding their philosophy of enterprise, their mindset disregards basic concepts like competitive advantage, target markets, customer service, and strategy.

The former U.S.S.R. and East Bloc communist nations remain the best empirical proof that this kind of Leninist experiment always ends in complete failure. Federal and state governments cannot decide which firms should be in a market, which should compete with whom, what prices should be charged, or how market shares are determined. Competition and opportunity should decide those. Private sector firms respond to demand from buyers. Each firm should plan product-service offerings, pricing, cost structure, and scale of operations based upon the market opportunity, and the potential to make a profit and build wealth. The central government mentality believes that politicians can legislate free market activities, with enough market share apportioned for each company to meet some baseline sales target, but not so much that one or more firms might dominate the others.

With regard to their zero-sum game perspective, every product-service market in the U.S. can be traced to its original form when the market was born from the initial entrant who innovated and

JOB CREATION

secured the first customers. Over time, the original firm was challenged on both features and price (or both), and a continuous string of advances ensued over the decades, always improving performance, putting downward pressure on prices, and increasing accessibility to a wider and wider user base. At some junctures, mergers and acquisitions consolidated some of the competitors. Sometimes the majority of firms adopted incremental change and the market moved in a new direction, leaving some companies out of the new trend. Yes, there are instances where a pioneering innovator introduced radical change, rendering most if not all of the market obsolete. That's how products and services improve over time, and all users benefit from improved performance and better prices. The notion that there can be no losers in a competitive market is entirely misguided. Rather, there can be no technological progress through quotas and price controls imposed by government planning and central orchestration.

The problem with these two lines of thinking is that when the government tries to manipulate the economy through central planning, resources are misappropriated and wasted, and no sustainable enterprises are ever created. In addition, there are no accrued benefits to entrepreneurs, business owners, shareholders, and employees. When the federal government takes increased business and individual tax dollars and funnels these into temporary programs for firms to complete a certain project, they call this job creation. But no job is actually created. No firms are launched. No innovation is leveraged. No competitive position is secured. Instead, government moves money to a fund that is then billed for cost of the project, including the wages for the temporary workers. There is no market plan, and no revenue gained to sustain the project. There is no profit targeted or earned. Benefits never accrue to those contracted for the project. When the project ends and the government funding dries up, the workers are again out of work and no real job creation happened. When the U.S. Census Bureau signed on 400,000 temporary

JOB CREATION

staffers to help complete the population count, the national unemployment statistics appeared to improve, but nothing was created, and no benefits accrued to any owners, investors, or employees. There were no sustainable new jobs created, only temporary paychecks funded by more federal debt. Yet this is what the government calls job creation.

For example, the government cannot decide in Washington that ethanol *will be* the next alternative energy of choice. The market will decide if a reasonable fuel can be produced relative to the costs of the corn and other raw materials, the manufacturing process, the distribution channels, and of course the performance in a wide range of vehicles. If it cannot compete with the ease of use, range of transportation, distribution, and cost of $3.00 per gallon gasoline, then Ethanol is NOT a viable product. When flash drives offered huge multiples of storage at fractional costs compared to CDs, the market adjusted – just as CDs had done to floppy disks in the previous innovation cycle. Why would anyone continue to use floppy disks when CDs were available? Why would anyone use CDs when flash drives came to market? To artificially prop up an industry or a company based upon thoughts of "equality" or "fairness" makes no sense. Politicians cannot legislate into existence innovative ideas, break-through technologies, or market structures. Similarly, government actions implementing early retirement, work sharing and tax credits won't boost employment; these all fall under the "lump of labor fallacy." (Bruce Bartlett, *How Not to Create Jobs*, FORBES (Feb. 19, 2010) http://www.forbes.com/2010/02/ 18/unemployment-minimum-wage-retirement-jobs-opinions-columnists-bruce-bartlett.html).

The unencumbered free market creates new firms, new products and services, and great new jobs, while government attempts at central planning only discourage market growth and job creation. But the federal and state politicians continue to pursue more intervention through higher taxes and spending programs, believing they can direct job creation and economic recovery that is planned, equitable, and parceled as what seems right to them.

JOB CREATION

Stimulus Funds & Federal Healthcare Don't Work

Two current government policies provide significant evidence that centrally planned federal spending programs cannot generate the same type of lasting employment opportunities as the private sector. The first, the *American Recovery and Reinvestment Actor 2009* (ARRA), was promoted by the Obama administration as the means by which Washington, DC would fix the US economy. The federal government allocated $800 billion to dozens of spending programs nationwide to supposedly create new jobs and spur economic growth. The second, the *Healthcare and Education Reconciliation Act of 2010* (HERA), is supposed to create all kinds of new jobs as the federal government enters the healthcare industry with layers and layers of regulations and oversight about who gets coverage, how much it costs, who has to pay for insurance and medical procedures, and who decides what is covered, all wrapped within an intricate matrix of fees, new taxes, and noncompliance penalties. If that's not bad enough, the primary billing and collection will be the responsibility of thousands of agents at the Internal Revenue Service.

Both ARRA and HERA are sadly, classic examples of how government views job creation. In the case of the former, the government doled out huge amounts of additional federal debt to temporary projects and, at the time the writing of this book was nearing completion, the funds were running out, no net new jobs were created, and local and state projects were scrambling to get a second round of stimulus funds approved to keep these temporary workers on the payroll for another few months (after which they will again be unemployed). In the case of the latter, the federal government is planning to jump right into the middle of the healthcare industry and unilaterally re-write the rules of competition, pricing, costs, service, and of course discourage any kind of profits. Again, nothing new is created, no lasting benefits are accrued, and no sustainable new jobs are created. The obvious problems with ARRA were massive increases in government

JOB CREATION

borrowing, combined with higher taxes and temporary work projects that only added to long-term inflationary pressures with rising interest rates that will result from the huge government deficits and runaway total debt. Stimulus packages typically do not work for the following five reasons.

- *Government spending packages frequently misdirect vital national resources away from the private sector capital markets.*

- *Stimulus packages don't increase aggregate consumption, but are simply re-directing existing consumption- no new value is generated.*

- *Stimulus packages don't create sustainable jobs – only temporary hiring for projects linked to the timeline of the funding allocations. When funding runs out, the projects cease, as do the associated jobs.*

- *Stimulus funds result in increased deficits, and therefore increase total national debt outstanding. These two are then major contributors to the propensity for rapid and prolonged inflation.*

- *Stimulus packages are generally pork-laden legislation with myriad levels of federal bureaucracy.*

Keynesian economics simply does not work. It is impossible to create wealth and sustainable economic growth in the economy by going into debt. Many of Keynes' disciples in Washington love to point to Roosevelt's *New Deal* as an empirical example of government-sponsored economic recovery. But, when Roosevelt tried stimulus spending to reduce the jobless rate during the 1930s, the results were very discouraging. "Despite Franklin Roosevelt's aggressive [federal] spending, unemployment reached 25 percent in 1933, fell only to 14 percent by 1937, and was back up to 19 percent in 1939. In the end, the New Deal did little or nothing to resuscitate the economy" (J.K. Glassman, *Stimulus: A*

JOB CREATION

History of Folly, Commentary Magazine [March 2009] http://www.commentary magazine.com/printarticle.cfm/stimulus--a-history-of-folly-14953). Critics of the Obama Administration's recovery acts are beginning to wonder if he is making the same mistakes as FDR. Large government, central planning, concessions to labor unions, and stimulus programs that FDR believed would produce jobs instead hiked the unemployment rate. Higher taxes certainly helped to divert significant capital away from the private sector and discouraged job creation by businesses. Writing for *Smart Money* (October 2008), Jonathan Hoenig noted: "The lesson is that a job is only useful when it fulfills an actual economic function, government creating jobs solely for the purpose of keeping constituents off the unemployment line simply misallocates scarce resources and prohibits actual jobs - productive jobs - from being developed in the private sector where they belong".

"Christina Romer [Obama's Chair for his Council of Economic Advisors] and Jared Bernstein, said U.S. unemployment would not go above 8% when [the] federal stimulus [bill] was enacted, yet the U.S. has had double-digit unemployment ever since (Bruce Bartlett, *Did the Stimulus Stimulate?*, FORBES (December 4, 2009) http://www.forbes.com/2009/12/03/tax-cuts-stimulus-jobs-opinions-columnists-bruce-bartlett.html). It is interesting that Ms. Romer states in her own research that government sponsored economic stimulus had virtually no effect on bringing the 1930s depression to an end. "Nearly all of the observed recovery of the US economy prior to 1942 was due to monetary expansion [as] huge gold inflows in the mid- and late-1930s swelled the U.S. money stock and appear to have stimulated the economy by lowering real interest rates, which encouraged investment spending and purchases of durable goods" (Romer, C. "What Ended the Great Depression?" 52 Journal of Economic History, No. 757 - 1992).

However, the stimulus is an example of the ineffectiveness of Washington's fiscal policies, as it consisted mainly of tax rebates.

JOB CREATION

Surveys revealed that rebates were either used to pay down existing debts, or were put away into savings, so the stimulus was ineffective because neither of these reactions directly generate lasting economic activity. *Consumer Expenditure Survey Results on the 2008 Economic Stimulus Payments (Tax Rebates)*, U.S. Dept. of Labor, Bureau of labor Statistics (October 15, 2009) http://www.bls.gov/cex/taxrebate.htm. For example, the Department of Labor reported that in April and May of 2010 new job creation continued to drop by 190,000 while stimulus money continued to pour into new projects. "These statistics reflected negatively on [the] stimulus package after the economy had lost roughly 2 million jobs since it was signed, and had fallen 7.2 million jobs short of [the] promised job creation projections" (*Morning Bell: Why Obama's Stimulus Failed*, THE FOUNDRY (June 7, 2010), http://blog.heritage.org/2010/06/ 07/morning-bell-why-obamas-stimulus-failed/).

Harvard economists Alberto Alesina and Silvia Ardagna studied dozens of examples of economic stimulus spending between 1970 and 2007 in 21 countries, including the U.S. and their findings are unequivocal. "Fiscal stimuli based upon tax cuts are more likely to increase growth than those based on spending increases; we would argue that the current stimulus package in the U.S. is too much tilted in the direction of [federal] spending rather than tax cuts; spending cuts are much more effective than tax increases in stabilizing debt and avoiding economic downturns, in fact, several episodes in which spending cuts [were] adopted to reduce deficits have been associated with economic expansions rather than recessions". At the start of the third quarter 2010, the June and July data continued to show a very weak job market, even as the first round of stimulus funds was running out – with no tangible evidence that more than three-quarters of a trillion dollars had done anything to spur economic activity and permanent new job creation. "Economists worry that the weak labor market will spook U.S. consumers, whose spending fuels the economy [so] [d]windling federal stimulus funds are only heightening those fears." (Alana Semuels, *With Federal Stimulus Funds Running out, Economic Worries Grow*, L.A. TIMES (June 30, 2010) http://articles.latimes.com/2010 /jun/30/business/la-fi-0630-stimulus-20100630).

The obvious problems with HERA are that no one really understands the specific organizational structure, processes, operations, and costs of how this law is supposed to function in the national market alongside America's existing healthcare providers and insurers. Some seventy percent of the Congress that voted for this bill now admits they have not read its provisions and do not know how it will function once it takes effect. So while Great Britain and Greece are working diligently to break away from the overwhelming failure of their federal health care programs, and to privatize former state-run systems, the U.S. – the world's leading capitalist, free market economy – is set to begin new legislation that will bring increased federal regulations, more government spending, higher taxes, additional fees and penalties for participating or not participating, and centrally planned oversight to this $1.2 trillion industry, serviced by some 600,000 firms, providers, and organizations, that represent around ten percent of U.S. annual GDP. Given the consistently poor track record involving fraud, budget overruns, deteriorating inefficient service, and increased costs of Medicare, federal welfare programs, Amtrak, The U.S. Postal Service, and other government programs, why should HERA be any different, especially given how little is known about how it will actually work once implement? Consider the extent of HERA's government planned intervention into the private sector. There are twelve recognized sectors within the U.S. economy:

- Basic Materials	- Capital Goods	- Financial
- Consumer Cyclical	- Consumer-Non Cyclical	- Energy
- Conglomerates	- Healthcare	- Services
- Technology	- Transportation	- Utilities

JOB CREATION

The Healthcare Sector is then comprised of twelve primary industries:

- Hospitals and Medical Facilities
- Medical Products + Instruments
- Health Maintenance Orgs (HMOs)
- Health Insurers/Healthcare Plans
- Pharmaceuticals + Drug Delivery
- Specialized Health Services
- Home Healthcare
- Hospital Management
- Long Term Care Facilities
- Medical Practitioners
- Biotechnology
- Medical Labs + Research

The federal government is going to get involved in virtually every aspect of the healthcare sector, and will initiate wholesale regulations imposed on how these industries will function in the future. HERA significantly alters, or even removes, the fundamental tenet of risk from the health insurance business model. The core model has always been based upon risk-transfer: where an insurer assesses a person's or entity's risk exposure to financial loss, and then charges a risk-premium for accepting all or a portion of that transferred risk. The premium is calculated based upon the insurer's ability to aggregate a wide range of risks into a large pool to diversify its overall exposure to the specific risks of any individual person or entity. Some relatively small percentage of the pool will require the majority of future financial payments, and these will come from the risk underwriter's proceeds that were charged to the pool. The much larger majority of the pool will experience much smaller or no financial needs, and yet will still enjoy the benefit of knowing their risk-exposure has been assumed by the underwriter. This is how it works for health insurance, auto insurance, disability-income insurance, homeowner's insurance, life insurance, and long-term care.

Private insurers will no longer be allowed to cap a limit on the amount of lifetime financial risk-exposure they must cover and pay benefits on, even though their premiums received will not be able to be raised to cover this increased risk exposure. Private

JOB CREATION

insurers can no longer drop coverage on a person's risk assumed when that risk becomes actuarially excessive relative to the financial capacity of the insurer to cover it. Private insurers must accept new individuals to the pool, even if they have a pre-existing condition that significantly negatively alters the insurer's ability to cover that risk. HERA's primary impact on job creation is that this legislation diverts large amounts of private sector capital resources away from consumer spending and company investments to pay for a wide variety of these altered risk-transfers that no longer function under typical risk-premium loss-exposure models. Higher taxes always mean less capital available for innovation, research + development, new asset investments, and new jobs. The most glaring negative impact is that $1 trillion of private individual and corporate capital is being legislatively mandated away from typical consumer spending, household investment, and capital-asset investment by companies in the private sector - into an entirely new centrally-planned, and centrally-managed federal government endeavor, and this will absolutely have a huge negative impact on private sector R+D spending, innovation, business expansion, and job creation at a time when America most needs tax relief to spur private sector investments and new hiring nationwide.

Disregarding the Certainty Factor

When government tries to legislate how the private sector functions, it literally disregards *The Certainty Factor*. Politicians fail to understand how business decisions are made about things like spending, borrowing, and investment. They disregard the private sector's need to see a strong degree of certainty in the economic near-term and beyond, and instead pursue policies that erode positive expectations for the future and create greater uncertainty. This disregard for individuals and businesses trying to make plans for R+D, new infrastructure, modernizing plant and equipment, investing capital, and borrowing new funds for inventory and other assets actually hurts job creation prospects.

JOB CREATION

As *The Certainty Factor* moves away from stable optimism toward the greater risk of increased volatility and pessimism, consumers are more hesitant to make significant purchases and businesses postpone or eliminate their plans to hire more workers. Yet the politicians cannot understand why individuals and companies in the private sector are resisting new borrowing and capital investments, so they continue to propose more and more regulations, federal programs, deficit spending, and higher taxes to try and pay for it all. But these actions only create more negative perspectives about their economic prospects for the future, further reducing job creation and other economic activity. Another round of tax hikes will only increase the overall financial burden on employees and employers. Once the government stimulus and spending stops, real job growth will emerge. (Newt Gingrich & Dan Varroney, *Stop the Insanity*, FORBES (December 31, 2009) http://www.forbes.com/forbes/2010/0118/opinions-einstein-debt-stimulus-on-my-mind.html).

The motivation for government policies regarding job creation is no doubt that the politicians truly want to see people going to work. But the political mindset is stuck – no, entrenched – in this "public sector rationale", completely at the expense of the private sector realities. Having never operated or managed a private sector business, they possess no sense about how borrowing, investment, and purchasing decisions are made. They cannot grasp that a company does not need help from the local, state, or federal government to pursue commercial opportunities. Politicians don't think about commerce and job creation with a view of profits, ROI, and building wealth. They disregard the core functions and tangible results of the private sector. They literally do not "get it" – that entrepreneurs and firms take risks in a competitive marketplace while vying for the same pool of buyers for their products and services, and so put people to work in a wide variety of jobs that are necessary to execute this commerce and be successful. As such, the current Democratic House, Senate, and President truly believe they can create new jobs through

JOB CREATION

legislation and a central plan conceived and implemented by government. In fact, their philosophical perspective is that regulatory initiatives are the best way to drive new employment.

This reasoning operates with the government as the catalyst for change and innovation, Subsequent "job creation" is a centrally-planned policy of the administration, where bureaucrats sit in committees and hearings, deciding where jobs will be created, and how many there will be by sector and industry across the economy. They supposedly have the intellectual credentials to formulate policies and lead the economy, but in reality, they don't "get it" at all, and instead implement legislative initiatives that actually introduce barriers to private sector job creation. Their thinking is short sighted and fundamentally flawed about what constitutes *creating* jobs. Increasing taxes on firms and individuals, then apportioning those tax dollars to government spending on programs that "hire" people for a limited-term project is not true job creation.

The Obama administration does not look to the resiliency of the U.S. economy as the initiator of new employment, but instead views the capitalist system as somehow inherently flawed in its ability to recover from recession, and in need of assistance from Washington. "What a productive, dynamic economy requires of a government is that it restrict itself to protecting property rights ... and refrain from interfering in free production and trade." (Yaron Brook, *To Stimulate the Economy, Liberate It*, FORBES (February 14, 2008), http://www.forbes.com/2008/02/14/yaron-economy-regulation-oped-cx_ybr_0214yaron.html). "More government spending, as many in Congress propose, will not reduce unemployment because government spending does not encourage businesses to invest and hire" (J. Sherk, *Unemployment Remains High Because Job Creation Has Yet to Recover*, THE HERITAGE FOUNDATION (June 4, 2010) http://www.heritage.org/research/reports/2010/06/ unemployment-remains-high-because-job-creation-has-yet-to-recover). In the next chapter we examine the

JOB CREATION

fundamentals of private sector wealth creation, and contrast it with government's insistence on pursuing policies aimed at systematic wealth redistribution. Such political posturing undermines the core rationales that drive private sector business development and job creation. So while espousing a seemingly politically correct egalitarian philosophy that should supposedly help everyone economically, the government actually cripples *The Certainty Factor* with numerous disincentives for profit and building wealth, and these directly puts job creation in jeopardy.

Chapter 5

Wealth Creation vs. Wealth Redistribution

> *"The primary goal of a market economy, driven by enlightened self-interest, is wealth creation that accrues to workers in the economy."*
>
> - Adam Smith 1776

The market economy is truly an amazing entity. Individuals, companies, and the government interact with each other on multiple levels of short-term, intermediate-term, and long-term transactions where millions of specific needs for products and services (aggregate demand) are met by tens of millions of specific product and service providers (aggregate supply). At the forefront of the market economy are several tenets that define the very basis for commercial enterprise. Smith rightly noted that individuals and companies exhibit an enlightened self-interest that provides the primary motivation for economic activities. It is a fascinating concept, because it is both "enlightened" and yet at the same time it's narrowly individualistic. Smith understood very clearly that there is a degree of inspiration, of moral accounting, and even responsibility, connoted in that enlightenment. That the pursuit of enterprise endeavors will ultimately benefit one's self is a refreshing concept. Too often though, politicians make the false assumption that pursuing self-interest is somehow not a positive exercise, but rather an inherently flawed rationale for venturing out into the market. This line of reasoning presumes that to there is some measure of corruption, greed, or exploitation of others

JOB CREATION

that will result from such action. Smith continued that creating new wealth should be both the primary goal and the natural outcome of enterprise and well it should be, and is. The opportunity to translate creative ingenuity and hard work into bettering one's life does not have to be inherently "selfish" (in the negative sense) while being self-interested. Starting up a business, with the potential for strong sales and a profitable bottom line, requires intrinsic motivation commensurate with the risk assumed in trying something new and untested. The creation of value where none existed prior to taking on risk is how markets get populated over time. Enterprise wealth then provides capital for other investments and financing throughout the market. At each juncture where wealth is created, new jobs are also created.

Lessons From Frank Knight

University of Chicago professor Knight championed the rationale that the risk-takers in the market engage in enterprising activities based upon the upside potential benefits that may accrue to them as compensation for having accepted the risk(s) of the commercial endeavor. His 1921 book, *Risk, Uncertainty, and Profit* remains a true classic about these three components of the American private enterprise system. First, risk is inherent is just about everything a person does throughout the day. Some things are very uncertain and questionable regarding their respective efforts and outcomes, and therefore present significant risks worth evaluating. Other activities are less ambiguous and as such have less risk, while certain prospects are easily understood and pose little if any risk. In each case, *The Certainty Factor* is intrinsic to some degree. Enterprise activity requires more than a risk-free environment. Entrepreneurs are agreeable to a wide variety of uncertainty provided there is acceptable potential upside reward matched to each successive increment of risk exposure.

Second, uncertainty is prevalent throughout all aspects of the private sector. That's what makes enterprise development such a

JOB CREATION

unique endeavor. Without a guarantee that the commercial venture will be successful, the vast majority of individuals opt out of entrepreneurial pursuits in favor of the greater certainty that comes with working for someone else and getting a regular paycheck. The risks cannot be completely eliminated, but certain aspects can be mitigated to some extent through planning and strategies for different outcomes. While the risk remains, the degree of uncertainty can be lessened and, at some point, the individual arrives at an acceptable degree of exposure that balances well in comparison to the upside rewards of the venture. The third facet in Knight's premise is the profit - that potential gain that will accrue to the owners as compensation for the risk assumed. Together, these define American private enterprise. Inherent risks are identified, uncertainty is reduced (certainty is increased) through careful planning, creativity, innovation, and strategy, and finally expected profit provides the motivation for executing the endeavor. As long as the profit potential compensates the individuals relative to the risk exposure and level of uncertainty for the outcome, individuals will continue to pursue new ideas for products and services in the free market. The wealth generation that ensues from enterprise development accrues to both owners and employees. Job creation is therefore the most natural outcome of such activities, with risk assumed by the owners, uncertainty reduced or accepted, and the motivation of an opportunity for profit driving the process.

The Wealth Creation - Wealth Redistribution Gap

We live in a world of limited resources and unlimited needs. Whether the problem we address is poverty, social injustice, economic growth, or job creation, the underlying issue is how to create the greatest prosperity for the largest number of people. While our free enterprise system has produced the wealthiest nation in history and has spread the benefits across a broad spectrum of the population, even capitalism's wealth creation potential cannot satisfy every individual's needs or cure all of

JOB CREATION

society's ills. Yet, by focusing on economic freedom and incentivizing individual achievement, free market capitalism works better than any other economic system ever devised. Socialism, and currently popular (and supposedly less oppressive) big government progressive economic theories, which promote the idea that governments can confiscate and redistribute an ever increasing percentage of the wealth their economies generate, are fatally flawed in one very significant respect: *Government confiscation and redistribution of wealth demeans the incentive to create wealth.*

The more a government confiscates and redistributes wealth so as to satisfy the needs of individuals other than those who created such wealth, the more it diminishes the incentive of those who create wealth. The destruction of individual incentives inevitably leads to a declining overall economy with an ever increasing number of people who feel entitled to government benefits, and an ever declining pool of resources from which the government can pay for such benefits. As such, over time, lacking an incentive for economic growth, socialist and big government progressive economies experience a decline in individual productivity, causing as overall economic decline, while increasing the need for government benefits at the very time the economy in general is shrinking, thereby reducing the wealth available to tax and pay for such government benefits. The flaw in such systems is comical at worst and grossly misguided at best.

What socialist agendas have always ignored, and what big government progressives in our nation increasingly ignore, is that every benefit provided by government to its citizens has a direct cost that the economy as a whole must bear. Governments take the monies from which they pay for such benefits by taxing wealth creation. Yet, all economies require wealth creation to subsidize government benefits. Eliminating the incentive to create wealth diminishes the pool from which governments can extract taxes to

JOB CREATION

pay for those benefits. Conversely, the more a government incentivizes individuals to retain the benefits of their labors, the greater the incentive to create wealth. The more wealth an economy generates, the larger the pool from which the government can extract taxes (confiscating wealth) without discouraging individual achievement. The need for government benefits diminishes as individuals become increasingly self sufficient, while simultaneously generating greater resources to help those in actual need as the economy grows and tax revenues increase. As such, socialist economies across the globe historically have provided their citizens incredibly meager, if not dismal, lifestyles (for example, Cuba, North Korea, pre-capitalist China, the former Soviet Union, and former Soviet bloc countries such as Poland and Hungry). These big government progressive economies incurred debts well in excess of their ability to pay, and therefore required a reduction in benefits for a citizenry that has come to believe it is *entitled* to such benefits (for example, Greece, Spain, Ireland, France, and Great Britain).

The reality is that economies must generate wealth far in excess of the benefits they provide, and free enterprise inevitably creates significantly greater wealth and prosperity across a much broader spectrum of the population than any system that is dependent on government confiscation and redistribution of wealth. Whether is it is universal health care, welfare, social security, Medicare or any other government sponsored benefits program - when the bills come due, someone must pay them. The only source the government has for payment is tax revenue and the true generator of tax revenue is private enterprise. Private enterprise is, in turn dependent on individual achievement. Not coincidentally, the most successful economies and those that provide the highest standard of living for their citizens are those that encourage individual achievement and wealth creation (for example, The United States (at least historically), Japan, Germany, Hong Kong, Singapore and, more recently, China). The flaw inherent in both socialist and big government progressive economies is the notion

JOB CREATION

that one can lift individuals and encourage achievement by taking wealth from those who are productive and giving it to those who are unproductive. In reality, the very government benefit programs socialists and big government progressives design to lift the individual are often equally (if not more) effective in discouraging individual achievement.

You cannot teach a man to fish by giving him a fish. You cannot instill the pride of accomplishing a task in people by accomplishing that task for them. You cannot foster in others a desire to achieve a goal by achieving that goal for them. Now, you can feel better about yourself and go about life believing you are a good and a giving person. Others may look up to you as a humanitarian and a charitable soul. But what have you really done other than delay the day when people will have to catch their own fish, accomplish their own tasks or set and achieve their own goals. Worse yet, you may be creating an entitlement attitude that causes the recipients of your largesse to expect fish without the effort of fishing. If no one provides the expected benefit, the result is generally resentment actually discouraging them from accomplishments or setting and achieving goals of their own. In reality, the greater the extent to which a government takes care of its citizens, the greater the potential that it will create a form of dependence. Under the guise of benevolence, such dependence empowers the individuals providing the care while emasculating the recipient. Few and far between are those individuals who will choose to work for what they can obtain without effort. Yet, accepting what you do not earn creates a dependence on the individuals or institutions providing for your needs. In this way, the welfare state creates dependent individuals always looking to the state to satisfy their need or desire for the things to which they have come to feel entitled.

This dependence empowers the class of individuals who control government benefit programs to dominate and control the lives of

JOB CREATION

the benefit recipients. Rather than having an economy that relies on those who produce wealth and prosperity, government dependence creates a ruling class consisting of those who control the confiscation and redistribution of wealth others have created. Since the individuals who create wealth no longer control the wealth they create, the incentive to continue creating wealth is extinguished. Private enterprise, on the other hand, instills in these same wealth-creating individuals the desire to accomplish their own tasks and achieve their own goals. It rewards those who expend the greatest effort and ingenuity. It creates opportunities for those seeking to control their own destinies and jobs for those who look for the security of employment and the satisfaction of earning what they achieve. Perhaps most importantly, it encourages all individuals to become productive wealth creators thus limiting the number of people in need of government benefits or dependent upon the government for their wellbeing. This is the very result those empowered by control of government benefit programs fight desperately to avoid. Individual incentive and responsibility are the antithesis of government power. Of course, there are those who genuinely need federal assistance. The elderly, the disabled, the infirm, the impoverished or those who, for reasons beyond their control, are unable to participate in the free enterprise system, should be able to rely on the generosity of those who can participate or the benefits the free enterprise system produces. However, where possible such programs should always seek to teach, educate or train in addition to simply providing benefits.

As noted above, a vibrant incentive driven economy will reduce the number of people dependent upon the government while increasing the pool of resources available to assist those genuinely in need. Problems arise not when government based programs aid those in need but rather when such programs entitle people to benefits they could earn themselves thereby removing the incentive to do so, depriving such individuals of the satisfaction and self worth that results from doing so. To the contrary, such

JOB CREATION

programs empower the government at the expense of the individual by creating dependence for such benefits. In other words, such programs reward destructive conduct (the expectation of benefits you have not earned) rather than productive conduct (earning and keeping the benefits you create). This empowers the government (and those who control it). Such empowerment leads to an increasingly larger bureaucracy as the government continues to increase in size to provide ever-expanding benefits to those who, through the ballot box, can empower the politicians who promise to expand their unearned government benefits.

The difficulty is that the government must have a source from which it can fund such benefits and that source is the tax revenue created by the individuals who work in the private sector. However, continuing to expand government benefits, as has been the case in the United States since the 1930s, serves to destroy the individual initiative to earn such benefits as individuals can obtain them by voting into power the party that promises to provide such benefits without the necessity of working for them. Why work to get what the government will give you if you vote for the right candidate? In this sense, government stifles individual initiative, retards economic growth, and hinders job creation. Yet, those whose careers are in government and those sympathetic to big government often come to view the government as a benevolent institution that lifts individuals by providing them benefits. In other words, the government helps such individuals by giving them fish instead of teaching them to fish. This government dependence leads to an ever increasing and powerful bureaucracy tasked with confiscating and redistributing wealth, expanding government's size, scope and cost. The end result is more intrusive and expensive, individual citizens who lack the incentive to be productive, a declining pool of resources from which to pay for the benefits such individuals now expect and a declining economy unable to provide employment opportunities for those who choose to work.

JOB CREATION

Reliance on big government is inherently destructive of individual initiative, economic growth and job creation. Free enterprise, on the other hands, takes the power to control wealth creation and distribution away from those who would confiscate and redistribute the wealth others have created and places that power in the hands of those who actually create the wealth in the first place. It incentivizes individuals to be productive as they will reap the benefits of their productivity thereby driving economic growth, reducing the number of individuals who need government assistance and increasing the size of the pool available to provide government benefits for those actually in need. The end result is economic growth, individual opportunity and organic job creation on a scale that socialists and big government progressives are unable even to contemplate.

Crippling The Certainty Factor

When politicians connive legislation to circumvent the private sector and install government at the center of the economy, believing they can take responsibility for growth, how much, by whom, for how long, and in what areas, they completely miss the detriment their actions are to strong private sector enterprise and job creation. Their mindset – that business profits are unnecessary or excessive and that wealth creation is synonymous with greed and exploitation – serves as the motivation behind increased regulations and higher taxes as the way to penalize individuals and companies for such economic gains. The idea that they can pass laws to orchestrate a smooth allocation of the nation's capital resources in a supposedly "fair" and rationed process is extremely naive. This distorted rationale advocates systematic wealth redistribution from those individuals and businesses deemed "rich enough", over to those they believe need their fair share of opportunity. The irony is that their efforts actually dissuade capital market activity, investment, enterprise, and job creation by fostering greater uncertainty about the future

JOB CREATION

prospects for economic gains. As such, *The Certainty Factor* is crippled, causing people and firms to stay on the sidelines waiting for a more positive and stable environment in which to make new purchases, borrow funds, invest capital, and create new jobs.

"An economy hampered by restrictive tax rates, will never produce enough revenue to balance our budget, just as it will never produce enough jobs or profits" (John F. Kennedy, Address to the Economic Club of New York [December 14, 1962] (transcript available at http://www.americanrhetoric.com/speeches/jfkeconomicclubaddress.html)). President Kennedy's timeless assessment could very well have been spoken in 2010 rather than fifty years ago in 1960. To paraphrase his insight, when an economy is burdened by excessive taxation and regulation, it increases the private sector's uncertainty about the future prospects for sustainable business opportunities, creating negative perspectives about hiring, drawing resources away from enterprising activities. Such an environment cannot produce sufficient tax revenues to balance the federal budget, nor enough jobs or business profits to improve the overall economy. "Government's consistent approach of increasing taxes on businesses and individuals with high income is profoundly detrimental to our economy; the reason being that entrepreneurs typically have higher incomes, therefore because small companies with fewer than 500 employees are responsible for the majority of new jobs, soaking the rich cripples job growth more than catalyzes it" ("Stimulating Failure", *Real Clear Markets* – November 7, 2009, http://www.realclearmarkets.com/articles/2009/11/07/stimulating_failure__97495.html).

In the prior chapter, we explained how government's definition of job creation actually disregards *The Certainty Factor* as the primary component of private sector decision making about future investments, borrowing, and purchases. In addition to that, the big government perspective of central planning and manipulation

JOB CREATION

of the economy through higher taxes and increased regulations goes one step further and severely cripples the *Certainty Factor*, by diminishing and even removing the enlightened self interest for individuals and businesses to pursue profits and build wealth over time. An interesting anecdote that illustrates this point involves my (Dave) 26 years of teaching at the college-university level. I have consistently engaged in conversations with students about what awaits them in the job market (and life in general) after graduation. I have also had this same conversation with my four children as they were in their college years. The dialogue always progresses from the bright hope and optimism about their opportunities still to come after they complete their degree, to a very frank enumeration of the realities of how individuals and government interact for the rest of one's adult life.

Our discussion of taxes always tops the list of students' profound disbelief that local, state, and federal government intrusion into their personal finances will be so pervasive. State income taxes, payroll taxes (FICA), federal income taxes, California SDI, sales taxes, gas taxes, required paperwork for annual state and IRS personal income taxes, capital gains taxes on any investments they'll make, property taxes on the home they hope to purchase someday – while walking them through that list, it never fails that their countenance and overall demeanor falls through several layers of dejection and general pessimism about their plans for the future. Add in all the taxes, fees, filings, regulations, and bureaucracy awaiting them if they start their own business (many of my entrepreneurship students do), and let's just say that their eyes glass over, and the crippling of *The Certainty Factor* presents itself very clearly in the shift to a tone of negative expectations about their future prospects. One resounding and consistent question has emerged over the years from these discussions: "So, how do you ever get ahead?" That's probably the great question on the minds of the vast majority of Americans as well. Government plans to redistribute private sector wealth completely miss the mark of even their flawed, intended

JOB CREATION

expectations for the economy, and in the end do more to significantly cripple *The Certainty Factor* at times when enterprise development and job creation are most needed.

Politicians believe they can literally sit at their legislative control panel and arbitrarily decide who has too much money, and then impose regulatory and tax penalties on these successful private sector participants to systematically move funds to individuals, firms, and social programs they have also arbitrarily decided are "deserving" of government's help through wealth transfer. This mindset is not to be taken lightly. The rationale is that injustice has occurred, allowing some to prosper while others are left out of economic gains, so government must correct this flaw in the private sector. "Leveling the playing field is often the mantra driving these funds transfers; governments neglect to realize that [such programs] don't inject new money into the economy, they just circulate [existing] funds." (Carroll, C. *Why the Stimulus Failed*, PHILADELPHIA BULLETIN - January 11, 2010, http://thebulletin.us/articles/2010/01/11/top_stories/doc4b4af8d1c8a61389824353.txt). Government sponsored wealth re-distribution cannot create new jobs or spark substantive gains in *The Certainty Factor*. This movement of existing funds is artificial, and fails to create any new wealth or gains in value from enterprising activities. The next chapter examines how primary job creation – making that new hire – actually happens in the private sector, and demonstrates *The Certainty Factor* in action.

Chapter 6

Primary Job Creation: The New Hire

> *"I have never hired a man or a woman based on a tax credit. Employers hire when they are certain they will have a growing market for their products; and they don't have that certainty now."*
>
> - Leo Hindery,
> InterMedia
> Partners, LP

The great majority of entrepreneurs begin by creating a job for just one person: themselves. Whether providing a service or a product, the initial question is whether there is sufficient market demand to justify one's own position in the endeavor before even considering the possibility of bringing in additional help. Yet, if a business is to grow, it will require more than a single person at the helm. Thinking back to chapter three, by adding employees the entrepreneur can multiply the business endeavor's overall productivity, reduce costs from economies of scale, improve the endeavor's ROI, and multiply the potential rewards from success. As such, the aggressive entrepreneur's goal invariably is to grow the venture by creating employment opportunities for qualified individuals who are unwilling to accept the risks of starting a business themselves, but who are willing to accept the security of a salary in exchange for their labors. Such new positions permit

JOB CREATION

the entrepreneur to expand the business, reap the benefits of a growing enterprise, and distribute to others a portion of the benefits from the venture's success. This is the nature of primary job creation which, when based on economic demand, generates self-sustaining employment and results in a growing, dynamic, and evolving economy.

Small businesses create around 60 to 80 percent of all new jobs in the U.S., and that drives our competitiveness. The ability of small firms to continue creating these new jobs is increasingly impacted negatively by their struggle to recover from the recession. Many firms put new hiring on hold when the economy is contracting, and they also cut existing jobs as a way to save on both direct labor costs and fixed overhead expenses until the economy and their sales recover. "The International Franchise Association (IFA) continues to impress on Congress a focus on policies that allow increased lending and limit government spending. Policies that increase lending help create long-term growth for the economy; therefore availability of credit is imperative to increased lending, and stability for small businesses and job creation." (Ken Walker, *Sound Regulatory Policies Are Needed to Spur Franchising Growth*, ALLBUSINESS.COM (June 14, 2010) http://www.allbusiness.com/franchises/14504975-1.html). This chapter focuses on primary job creation, namely, that management decision to open up a new position within the firm based upon strong positive signals about sales and market growth, and profit potential.

Hiring Is A Business Decision

In many ways, this section of the book could be published as a small 15-page booklet titled: "How To Make A Job". Copies of this pocket reference guide could be distributed throughout public and private schools nationwide. Children as young as middle school could easily grasp the simple principles of American private enterprise and how the decision to hire new workers is actually

JOB CREATION

made. Perhaps copies could also be handed off to all state legislatures, governors, the Congress, and the White House – easy reading that if implemented, would have a profound positive impact on creating new jobs and sparking our economy on to recovery. The key principle on the first page would state concisely (and obviously) that: *Government NEVER Creates Jobs, Because Hiring Is A Business Decision!*

The ability to correctly assess whether to make a new hire is an attribute of both owners and senior managers, and it is essential to the overall success of any business. Three key aspects of hiring a new employee are (1) the decision on which positions to add, (2) how much compensation to offer, and (3) the determination as to whether you have the right employee for that position. An employer generally makes the decision to create a new position based on two simple questions: 1) Do I need someone to fill this role; and, 2) Can the business afford it? While an entrepreneur initially may be able to handle the needs of the enterprise on his or her own, or with a few employees, the reality is that as the company grows over time, the need for specific skill sets in areas such as production, sales, operations, marketing, finance, and accounting often reach beyond the entrepreneur's abilities and available time. To survive and grow, the business will need additional direct hires to fulfill the various roles necessary to operate successfully. Having the ability to make a high quality product is not the same as having the ability to sell that product. Having the ability to sell a product is not the same as having the ability to impose on your business the financial discipline necessary to make the enterprise profitable.

To satisfy the needs of a growing business, the entrepreneur must reach out directly to individuals with the required skill sets, or else the business will lose its competitive edge, stagnate, and eventually fail. For example, let's assume that an entrepreneur who is skilled at making furniture starts a furniture business. An

JOB CREATION

individual skilled at making furniture may lack the sales or financial skills necessary to create a demand for products or to grow the business. If the business does expand, it will require bookkeepers, sales people, and additional trained furniture makers to maintain its success and growth. The entrepreneur's role is to analyze the needs of the business, determine which roles he or she can satisfactorily fill with current staff, and then hire qualified individuals to fill those the existing staff is unable to handle. The entrepreneur must also look to what the competition is doing. If the competition is providing superior service or producing superior products at a competitive price, the entrepreneur may need to add employees or replace current workers to improve the enterprise's services or products. Making the correct decisions in this respect leads to profitability and growth. The wrong decisions about the work force can doom the venture before it ever gets off the ground.

Growth is the key to continued job creation. The entrepreneur is constantly in the position of having to decide whether to create a new position to service an expanding business, to operate with existing staff, or to cut costs by reducing the employee head count. If the business is to succeed, the entrepreneur must base this decision on the needs of that business. Overstaffing a firm can be as dramatic a mistake as understaffing. The growth potential of a business and the demand for products or services will out of necessity drive the hiring decision. The desire to generate greater revenues and profits will push the entrepreneur to constantly expand naturally, and increase the need for more skilled employees, who in turn will further enhance the growth potential of the enterprise.

This entrepreneurial drive toward an ever-expanding base of new employees is at the heart of the free enterprise system's job creation engine. Because growth is generally the key to increased profits and direct hires are the key to growth, there is constant internal pressure to assess, locate, and add profit-enhancing new

JOB CREATION

positions. Conversely, because overstaffing leads to decreased profitability (which inhibits growth), there is a built in fail safe against overreaching and undermining the business.

This entrepreneurially driven process is the antithesis of government job creation. Governments design jobs to fit within budgets intended to accomplish specific tasks. The more people available to accomplish the task, the easier it is for each of the government employees involved in completing such tasks. That is to say, the less they have to work. There is no overriding need to make a profit, develop, grow, or maintain a competitive advantage. The government generally lacks a profit incentive and has no competition. Consider the functional malaise of the U.S. Postal Service, The Department of Motor Vehicles, Amtrak, or the Small Business Administration. The tenets and rationales that drive primary job creation in the private sector do not apply to these entities. Hiring in these organizations is simply a function of government budget appropriations. There is little, if any, attention given to customers, revenue, or profit growth associated with adding new workers. Accomplishing a given task itself does not increase the government's economic viability, solidify the employee's job security, or justify additional hires. The decision to add additional direct hires is a reflection of how much work there is to do, how much is currently getting done, and how much money is budgeted to the task. Employee inefficiency will generally increase the need for additional employees thereby further easing the workload on existing employees. The incentives to be productive are limited.

For example, assume a private firm could issue drivers' licenses. In a competitive environment, if there were 1,000 drivers' license applications to process in a day and the firm had four employees who were each processing 200 per day, the business would need another employee to meet the daily volume, or the four existing employees would need to increase productivity to 250 per day. The entrepreneur would base the decision to add that fifth direct

JOB CREATION

hire on whether there were clear ways to incentivize the four existing employees to increase their productivity, or were they already working at their maximum capacity. This decision would also depend on how the competition was balancing labor costs and productivity. If neither the entrepreneur nor the competition could process the required number of applications profitably, they would raise prices to offset the necessary expense of an additional hire. If one competitor was unable to get the required productivity, or hire additional workers while maintaining profitability, that firm would eventually fail. So there are very real incentives to help make existing employees productive, and to add workers if the functional needs of the firm require such.

Having the government process drivers' licenses changes the entire scenario. The incentives for the four employees to work harder are limited. Lacking an incentive to maximize employee efficiency, harder work generally will result in resentment from co-workers who prefer to work less diligently, rather than an increase in salary or a positive impact on the survival of the enterprise. If there are 1,000 applications to process in a day and the team only processes 800, there is really nowhere else to go for the people whose applications the government employees failed to process on that day. The government has no competition. If the government employees accomplish less than 100% of the job at hand, there is neither a corresponding loss of business nor an economic benefit from processing all 1,000 applications. The incentive to make additional direct hires and thereby increase efficiency to remain competitive is literally non-existent. Moreover, there is no guarantee that adding employees will increase efficiency as there is little motivation for such employees to be efficient. The government already has 100% of the market for this product-service application and can service that space at a low level of efficiency within a limited budget, without any risk of losing customers or going out of business.

JOB CREATION

Because the basis for making the hiring decision is very different for entrepreneurs compared to government officials, the impact on the overall economy is also very different. By necessity, when an entrepreneur makes a decision to hire an employee in the private sector, it is because the owner perceives the employee's productivity will exceed the cost of having that new worker on the payroll. In other words, the new hire will contribute to the profitability of the business venture and facilitate its growth. It is a decision driven by economic factors and, if the entrepreneur analyzes those factors correctly, the decision to hire should lead to a self-sustaining position for the longer term. As such, making the decision to hire a new employee in the private sector involves a constant evaluation and re-evaluation of what will drive economic growth at the most basic level. Government hiring lacks a similar economically motivated driving force. Rather, when government enters into a business formerly in the private sector, the underlying economic motivation towards sustainable economic growth is simply absent when making a hiring decision. As such, the driving force behind sustainable job creation is also lost. In the end, it's a clear and rational business decision to hire a new worker, and that defines primary job creation.

Unlike government hiring, in the private sector, the desire to increase profits drives the decision whether to create new jobs. Increased demand for your product or service creates the opportunity to increase the number of individuals you employ. This, in turn, increases your total revenue as you are producing and selling more products or serving more customers. Assuming you are making a profit on the products you sell or the services you provide, increasing your production and revenue should increase your total revenue and the profits you bring to the bottom line. Additionally, increasing your total revenue reduces the percentage of such revenue attributable to your fixed expenses (costs that do not change as your revenue increases) and semi-fixed expenses (costs that increase at a slower rate than your revenue). This reduction in costs as a percentage of total revenue

JOB CREATION

results in a leveraging of your fixed and semi-fixed expenses against your revenues increasing your profits as a percentage of total revenue thereby further increasing the total dollars you bring to the bottom line, i.e., your profits. As the examples below demonstrate, this sounds more complicated than it is. Nonetheless, the end result is that creating jobs in a profitable private sector business both improves the productivity of such business and lowers its operating costs as a percentage of total revenue, both of which increase profits.

For example, if a firm produces a product (widgets) at a facility large enough to accommodate additional employees and increased production, even as the company improves revenues, the rent (a fixed expense) stays the same. If that rent is $1,000 per month with five employees making 100 widgets total per month, the firm needs $10 in revenue each month per widget just to cover the rent. If total expenses including rent are $20 per widget, the firm must sell widgets for an amount in excess of $20 to make a profit. Let's assume the company sells widgets for $25 each. With 100 widgets per month, profits are $500 ($5 on each unit, times 100 widgets). If that same facility can house ten employees who make 200 widgets per month, the firm will only need $5 in revenue per widget to cover the $1,000 in rent each month. If widgets can sell for $25, the firm now makes not only the original $5 per widget for a total of $1,000 (doubling profits as the firm doubled employees and production), but now the firm also has increased profits per widget by an additional $5. This means the firm needs fewer dollars per widget to cover the fixed rental obligation of $1,000 per month. As such, the enterprise now makes $2,000 per month consisting of: 1) the original $5 profit per widget doubling to $1,000 per month as production doubled, plus 2) the additional $1,000 per month saved due to the reduction in the amount needed per widget to cover the rent expense. As such, the firm quadrupled the profit, but only doubled the employees from five to ten, while production also doubled from 100 to 200. Assuming there are competitors making widgets, the firm could also lower

JOB CREATION

the price of widgets from $25 to $22.50 and still make the same $5 per widget made prior to doubling the workforce. This would include an additional $2.50 ($5 in rent savings less $2.50 in price reduction) for a total of $1,500 in profit from 200 widgets, which is triple what the firm produced before doubling the total employment base.

In other words, by doubling employees and creating those new jobs, the firm dramatically increased profits. This occurred because the company is now manufacturing more widgets (increasing productivity and total revenue), and because fixed and semi-fixed expenses on that revenue declined as a percentage of total revenue. This further increased overall profitability on each widget produced providing the option to either keep a greater portion of a larger revenue base, or reduce prices making the product more competitive as circumstances in the market may dictate. In any event, by adding jobs, the firm increased total production, reduced expenses, and thereby enhanced both profitability and its competitive position in the marketplace.

A similar analysis applies in the service industry. For example, a lawyer who bills $150 per hour for his services and bills and collects for two thousand hours per year (not a simple task), will have gross revenues of $300,000 per year. Assuming overhead expenses are 50% of revenue, he will make $150,000 per year before taxes. This attorney will be unable to increase the clients he serves or his overall billings, as his hours are limited. His sole product is his time. In effect, he has capped his own earnings potential by being the only revenue producer. However, if this same attorney is able to generate more business than he can service himself (the legal profession calls him a "rainmaker"), he can increase his profits by hiring additional attorneys to the firm. If he hires four additional attorneys to work for him, and they each charge $150 per hour (and bill and collect two thousand hours per year), the five attorneys generate combined annual revenue of $1.5 million. This attorney already has fixed expenses (rent,

JOB CREATION

receptionist, secretary, access to research materials and case law). He will also have certain increased expenses essentially to cover salaries, increased administrative help, and possibly increased rent to cover additional space for the new attorneys. Assuming that he pays the newly hired attorneys $100,000 each, and that his overhead stays at 50% of revenue (which should not be the case as discussed below), he will now make the $150,000 he was already making plus $50,000 from each of the additional four attorneys he hired. That $200,000 in additional marginal profit is the result of the $300,000 he collects for each of their services, less the $100,000 he pays them in salary, less the $150,000 attributable to overhead expenses at 50% of revenue. This results in income for the attorney of $350,000 (4 x $50,000 plus $150,000). As certain of his expenses were fixed or semi-fixed and did not increase, he should have an additional benefit to his bottom-line profit. Let's say his overhead expenses are now only 40% of revenue, because he did not need another receptionist, he already had certain administrative help, and he only needed minimal additional office space for the new attorneys he hired.

Five attorneys at $300,000 per year generate $1.5 million in revenue. Assuming expenses are 40%, this leaves $900,000 before paying the attorneys their $400,000 in combined salaries, leaving the owner $500,000 per year - over three times what he was making on his own. From a competitive standpoint, this should also free the attorney- entrepreneur to do what he does best - generate new business. If he spends 50% of his time on non-billable client generating tasks, and reduces his personal earnings (his billable hours) from $150,000 to just $75,000, he still makes $425,000 total per year – three times what he made on his own. Spending more time on client development will further enhance his ability to bring in more business, hire more attorneys, further reduce his fixed and semi-fixed expenses as a percentage of his revenue, and continue to increase his profits.

JOB CREATION

The restaurant business is another good example of how job creation can increase production while reducing costs. A typical quick service restaurant, for example, is a fixed size and gives its customers the option of eating in the restaurant, ordering food to take out, or ordering through the drive-thru. As business increases, there comes a point at which the restaurant requires additional employees (cooks, counter people, servers) to maintain the appropriate levels of food quality, service, and cleanliness. In this case the entrepreneur is attempting to assure that he has adequate staff to prepare the food (production) as well as adequate staff to assure a positive experience for his customers (service). Obviously, the more food he sells, and the more often customers return to make repeat purchases, the more profit his business will earn.

A restaurant doing $1 million per year in revenue will have four basic categories of expenses: 1) food and paper, 2) labor, 3) occupancy, and 4) advertising. Let's say these expenses total 85% of revenue. The restaurant level profit for this $1 million unit would then be $150,000 (15% after expenses). As business increases to $1.25 million per year, certain direct costs will increase (for example food and paper costs) at about the same rate as total revenue increases. However other expenses either stay the same in real dollars, or increase at a lower rate. Occupancy is a good example of a fixed expense that remains the same in real dollars, but becomes a lower percentage of revenue as business increases. This assumes the restaurant operator either owns the site or has a fixed rent (as opposed to rent set as a percentage of the unit's revenue). Given the prevalence of take-out and drive-thru orders, it is unlikely that increased revenue will quickly lead to a need for more space and higher rent. While rent is good to use for demonstrative purposes, other expenses also remain unchanged in real dollars or increase only slightly. The building needs to be heated or cooled no matter the number of customers served or the number of employees. The lights are on whether the restaurant is doing $1 million in business or $1.25 million -

JOB CREATION

whether there are 25 employees or 30 employees. Thus, as revenues increase, expenses in addition to rent will remain constant in real dollars or increase only slightly while declining as a percentage of total revenue. This increases both the restaurant's profit margin and the overall bottom line.

The restaurant operator will invariably add staff as sales increase. It is simply impossible to maintain and grow the customer base absent the ability to make the food and provide a positive experience. However, in this example, labor becomes a semi-fixed expense because labor will increase at a lower rate than revenue increases because there is a range within which a staff of people can adequately service the restaurant's customers. For example, a staff that can handle $1 million per year in business should be able to handle an increase to $1.1 million without adding more workers. Nonetheless, as business increases, if the operator wants to continue to grow, additional employees will be needed to assure they can make the food in a timely manner (production) while also maintaining food quality, service, and cleanliness. The successful restaurant operator will always be looking to assure that he has the right number of employees in the restaurant at any given time to guarantee a positive experience for the customers. Larger restaurant chains have very sophisticated formulas and computer programs to assist restaurant managers in maintaining the right number of people in the restaurant at any given time.

As the restaurant operators' revenues increase by 25% to $1.25 million, he will need to add employees. If fixed and semi-fixed expenses were to remain stagnant as a percentage of revenue, profits would also remain stagnant as a percentage of revenue. Think back to the prior example. With expenses totaling 85% of revenue, the restaurant operator's profits at 15% of $1.25 million would be $187,500 - about 25% more profit than the $150,000 made on the $1 million. In other words, revenues increased at the same rate as profits (25%) because expenses remained a constant percentage of revenue (15%).

JOB CREATION

However, as noted, certain expenses will not remain the same. Leveraging fixed and semi-fixed expenses against increased revenue results in profits increasing at a higher rate than revenue. With many costs staying the same or increasing only marginally as revenue increase, despite adding more workers, our restaurant operator lowers expenses as a percentage of revenue. Let's assume a five percentage-point reduction in total expenses due to fixed and semi-fixed expense reductions, resulting in a decline in total expenses to just 80% of revenue. This results in profit margins increasing from 15% to 20% - now $250,000 or a 66% improvement with only a 25% increase in revenue.

In every one of these examples, hiring is clearly a business decision based on the entrepreneur's desire to increase profits. In each of these examples, we made no adjustments for increases in taxes or the cost of burdensome regulations or government mandates. Obviously, such increased expenses would reduce the profitability of adding new employees and thereby reduce the entrepreneur's motivation to add them. In the private sector, unlike the government, hiring is profit-based. While there is an inherent motivation in the private sector to increase revenues, hire new employees, and leverage fixed and semi fixed expenses to improve profitability, adverse government actions can offset this motivation and discourage both job creation and economic prosperity. If politicians understood how managers and owners think through the decision to add new workers, they would recognize how important it is to assist the private sector by creating economic and political certainty. In this way, *The Certainty Factor,* provides the motivation and risk-reduction necessary to promote robust job creation. Rather than temporary government program jobs funded by higher taxes and deficit spending,. these jobs will be regular new additions to a company's operating plan, and tied to plans for expansion, growth in sales, and higher profits. Whether a business provides services or manufactures products, with a growing market opportunity and the entrepreneur's ability to manage growth successfully,

JOB CREATION

increasing production by hiring more employees will invariably increase revenue, while also reducing costs as a percentage of revenue, and improve profits. This profit driven nature of the free enterprise system inherently incentivizes entrepreneurs to create new jobs because they result in increased productivity, reduced costs, better profits, and value-added wealth accrued. The free enterprise system has an inherent bias for job creation. On the other hand, government simply does not work this way. Trying to involve politicians in the job creation process through increased taxation and regulation always reduces or eliminates the core profit motive, which is essential to sustainable job growth.

Value-Added to Companies & Employees

Creating permanent jobs and retaining long term employees is a great value added proposition for both employers and employees. In exchange for their services and loyalty, employees receive compensation and the satisfaction that comes from supporting yourself and your family, being part of a successful enterprise, and effectively completing your tasks. For taking the risks inherent in any business venture and creating the jobs associated with that venture, the employer/entrepreneur earns the profits the enterprise generates and has the satisfaction that comes from creating an enterprise and making it successful. Ideally, this is the most equitable of trades.

This mutual benefit is essential to the success of our free enterprise system because it organically generates the energy necessary to grow our economy and create jobs. Unfortunately, there have been instances in our history when powerful employers took advantage of and exploited their employees. Congress has at various times enacted legislation to address employer abuses such as the laws prohibiting child labor or creating the 40-hour workweek and the minimum wage. There have also been instances where powerful labor unions have

JOB CREATION

abused employers driving labor costs so high that the companies were unable to remain competitive (for example, most recently, General Motors and Chrysler) resulting in entire industries becoming uncompetitive and all but vanishing along with the jobs such industries created (e.g. the domestic clothes manufacturing industry). Yet, these examples of oppressive counterproductive practices by large employers and powerful labor unions mask the true mutually beneficial relationship between employer and employee more prevalent in our history and our current economy. The reality is that the free enterprise system by its very nature encourages employers to value their employees and encourages employees to work to their maximum potential so that both enhance the value of their mutual endeavors.

There is the obvious benefit to the employer from a profit perspective in creating a new job in the first place. That benefit is enhanced over time as the employee gains experience in the position enhancing his knowledge base and enabling him to perform at a higher level. This allows the employer to produce a higher quality product or provide a superior service more cost effectively. Long-term employees also eliminate the need for the employer to incur hiring and training costs to replace such employee and may actually reduce the training cost for additional employees who they can assist in training. As such, the long-term employee in a productive self-sustaining job is an extremely valuable asset to the enterprise and one the intelligent employer/entrepreneur will protect and encourage.

Similarly, there are obvious benefits to the employee who holds a self-sustaining profit producing job. The most obvious benefit is a continuing income stream or, more simply, a salary and benefits that improve the employee's lifestyle and increase the employee's personal wealth. As the employee's skill set improves and his knowledge with respect to how best to perform his function increases over time, he becomes more efficient and productive

JOB CREATION

justifying a salary increase and potentially a promotion. In addition, the employee may be entitled to benefits such as stock options that increase in value over time if the enterprise is profitable, allowing the employee to participate in the venture's success. In addition, the benefits of being a part of a successful growing enterprise, of performing a job to the best of your abilities, of supporting yourself and your family and of accomplishing your goals are immeasurable.

This overlapping of mutual benefits makes the system work. Each side energized to be productive. The risk taker seeking the rewards you only get from taking risks and the person seeking the security of a job, a ladder to climb with limited personal risk, both incentivized to succeed. This dynamic drives the enterprise to achieve. This is far different from systems where a minority with power based on heredity or political clout, has an employee base that is compelled to work a government job where superior performance has limited benefits and retirement with a government pension is the goal. Private enterprise job creation also accrues a series of tangible gains to both employers and the employees. The successful entrepreneur has one primary objective: to increase profits over time. The opening chapter to just about every microeconomics, accounting, and corporate finance textbook states this axiom: *the focus of the firm is to increase shareholder wealth.* Sustainable and growing profits over time translate into greater value for the enterprise. This value is reflected in the equity section of the balance sheet in the form of net worth. It is also evident for public companies in the price of the common stock on the market.

While these tangible gains accrue to owners and increase the value of the current and fixed assets (which in turn continue to generate revenue for operating costs), the employees also accrue tangible gains in the form of disposable income earned from the salaries and hourly wages paid by the employer. This cash flow

JOB CREATION

works for the individual household in much the same way revenue works for the firm. Households use the steady, reliable income earned to pay for direct living expenses (housing, utilities, food, transportation, insurance, taxes), after which the remaining discretionary income is available for a wide range of purchases, including entertainment, clothing, household goods, vacations, as well as various investments.

Over time, pay increases allow households to make additional purchases, borrowing, savings, and investments throughout the economy. Employees may also have some means to obtain equity in their own company through some form of stock purchase plan, options and/or shares granted as a bonus, or as part of a retirement plan. Having a vested interest in the wealth creation of the business can then result in: 1) the accumulation of personal assets such as a home, automobiles, savings accounts, investments, retirement accounts (401k, IRA, 403b, profit-sharing), and 2) participation in the aggregate wealth accumulation of the firm as it gains value over time. This value-added component of primary job creation is often lost on the federal government. Individuals and companies that are generating income and profits then provide through those cash flows the savings and investment funds that supply the broader capital markets. This in turn helps make credit more available – both business lines and personal/household credit cards and loans on cars and other large purchases.

Having strong and identifiable value-added benefits accrue to both firms and individuals is another hallmark of the American capitalist system. There is no need for the local, state, or federal governments to be involved in this process. The free flow of funds from buyers to the firms in the form of sales provides the necessary funds to meet payrolls, which put more money into the hands of individuals and households in the economy. These then purchase, save, and invest. The firms expand to meet stronger demand, and the savings and investments provide additional capital market funding for financial intermediaries to support

JOB CREATION

businesses as they grow. The reliability of employment contributes to a favorable *Certainty Factor* for individuals and households in the economy. Strong certainty about having a job, getting paid regularly, and the prospects for consistently receiving a bonus and/or pay raises over time provide the positive perspective that guides larger purchases and investments, like a new home, remodeling one's existing home, taking a luxury vacation, and buying big-ticket durable goods like cars or major appliances. So too, *The Certainty Factor* improves for businesses as well when the private sector's flow of funds functions with less intrusion from government regulations and taxes. Value-added wealth creation from successful enterprise puts more money in the hands of both firms and households, and contributes to an optimistic future perspective.

The Certainty Factor and Hiring

Primary job creation depends on *The Certainty Factor*. Entrepreneurs and senior managers at large companies both view the hiring decision relative to the expected future environment, and the directly related prospects for sales and profits. It may sound overly simplistic, but the core rationale remains undeniable. When federal regulations are being reduced or eliminated, government spending is reined in, and taxes are lowered across the board, individuals and businesses perceive a greater degree of certainty about their prospects for personal income and company profits. This increased certainty generates stronger optimism about taking business risks and pursuing new market opportunities. Individuals and firms have a more positive outlook for their own financial situations, and the economy overall. This translates into pulling the trigger on expansion plans, making new purchases, modernizing plant and equipment, borrowing funds, and investing. If business owners, entrepreneurs, and senior managers at large corporations forecast greater certainty about the economic landscape regarding interest rates, the money supply, inflation, the strength of the dollar against foreign

JOB CREATION

currencies, consumer confidence, and related measures, the risks associated with venture plans is reduced, and it's a great time to grow and hire more workers.

At the time this book was in process, here in California, certain bumper stickers in support of Jerry Brown for governor stated: "Let's Get California Working Again". At face value that seems like a fairly straightforward goal. But California's state government spending has a $19 billion deficit and unemployment is at 12.6% - third highest in the nation. Entrepreneurs and large companies alike, from San Diego, Orange County, Los Angeles, the Central Coast, and up through the Bay Area and Silicon Valley, have clearly interpreted the current *Certainty Factor* to be extremely unpredictable and anything but certain. This negative perspective on the future prospects in our state due to increasingly higher taxes, more fees, and additional government regulations calls into question any plans to expand, make new purchases, modernize, and of course, hire new workers.

Politicians have been taking numerous photo-opportunity PR-tours of California solar panel manufacturing plants in an effort to generate a positive outlook for this industry and new jobs that might follow its expansion. But the only reason these would improve *The Certainty Factor* is if these panels are truly a competitive alternative energy product in the market, with strong demand coming from all segments of residential housing and commercial real estate. If the cost of buying and installing solar panels does not make economic sense relative to traditional energy media and costs, then demand will not drive this emerging fringe industry into the mainstream of the California and national economies. Pessimism about federal and state tax credits as incentives to "go solar" keep aspects of *The Certainty Factor* for this industry mixed at best. Venture capital, angel investors, and banks are still hesitant to make significant investment commitments to solar. As such, job creation in this industry has not shown promising signs of taking off anytime soon.

JOB CREATION

If personal incomes were expected to rise with lower sales taxes and income taxes, and business profits were also projected to be very strong due to cuts in corporate tax rates and further reductions – or better yet, elimination of – capital gains taxes, the overall outlook for the future would move toward better certainty, and, assuming consumer demand for solar panels, more individuals and firms would make financial commitments to developing, manufacturing, and selling/installing the next generation of highly efficient, low cost solar energy solutions throughout the state. That kind of groundswell optimism would kick start significant job creation as new plants would open and require a wide range of production workers; R+D would expand and require specially-trained workers to pursue innovative product development; new installations would begin to ramp-up requiring an army of trucks and vans with skilled workers to get these panels on rooftops; and service contracts would require more and more maintenance technicians and customer support reps to back the expanding market.

Companies that create new jobs, expand their overall production output of goods and/or services. This increased capacity for manufacturing and servicing new customers shows up on the balance sheet in the form of improved inventory and cash flow as part of current assets, and in new client contracts and accumulated goodwill as part of fixed assets. In addition, expanded operations will translate into more funds allocated to R+D, equipment, machinery, and overall physical plant, also as part of fixed assets. These fixed assets form the primary bases that generate revenue to the firm in the form of sales on those products and services created by the expanded work force. After deducting the variable costs of labor and materials, the fixed overhead expenses, interest on debt, and provisions for income taxes, the company shows its profit on the bottom line. Throughout the fiscal year, businesses make a wide range of investments from the cash flow on their income statement, including new equipment and machinery, provisions for expanded

JOB CREATION

inventory, and the additional hiring of all kinds of new employees. These each add to the business's assets (both current and fixed), and these gains in asset values show up on the right side of the balance sheet as increases to retained earnings. In the short term, the various factors of production improve the company's internal capabilities to deliver goods and services to the targeted market, and service that expanding customer base over time. The hiring decision flows directly from these kinds of activities. But what of the kinds of policies, programs, regulations, and taxes that disregard and even cripple *The Certainty Factor*? The following narrative provides a direct insight into the mind of a real business owner assessing his own *Certainty Factor*, confounded by the excessive role government has developed in decreasing his optimism and fueling a negative perspective.

Michael Fleischer examined the painstaking process of one company's analysis about employment, and how increased uncertainty hurts plans for future new hiring. (M. Fleischer, *Why I'm Not Hiring*, WALL STREET JOURNAL (August 9, 2010) http://online.wsj.com/article/ SB10001424052748704017904 575409733776372738.html). "With unemployment at 10% and companies sitting on their cash, you would think that sooner or later job growth would take off. I think it's going to be later - much later, and here's why. Meet Sally, one of the 83 people at my small business in New Jersey. She's been with us 15 years and makes $59,000 annually (on paper). In reality, she makes only $44,000 because $15,000 is taken from her thanks to various deductions and taxes. Before any money hits her bank, it is reduced by the $2,376 she pays as her share of the medical and dental insurance that my firm provides. Then the government takes $126 for state unemployment insurance, $149 for disability insurance, and $856 for Medicare. That's the small stuff. New Jersey then takes $1,893 in state income taxes. The federal government gets another $3,661 for Social Security, and then comes $6,250 for IRS income tax withholding. The roughly $13,000 [confiscated] by these various government entities

JOB CREATION

means that 22% of her gross pay goes to Washington or Trenton. She's lucky she doesn't live in New York City, where the toll would be higher with a city income tax."

He continues. "Employing Sally costs my company plenty too. We write checks totaling $74,000 so she can eventually receive her nominal $59,000 in pay. Health insurance is a big added cost - Sally pays $2,400 and I pay the rest - $9,561. We also provide life insurance and other insurance premiums amounting to $153. Together, company-paid benefits add $9,714 to my cost of employing her. The federal government takes another $56 for unemployment tax, $149 for disability insurance, $300 for workers' compensation, and then $505 for state unemployment insurance. Finally, the IRS makes me pay $856 for Medicare and $3,661 for Social Security. When you add it up, it costs $74,000 to put $44,000 in Sally's pocket, and to give her $12,000 in benefits. Bottom line: governments together impose a 33% surtax on Sally's job. Because my [firm] has been conscripted by the government and forced to serve as a tax collector, we have lost control of a big chunk of our [internal] cost structure."

Tax increases dramatically alter every company's financial situation. With increased government spending, deficits growing by well over $1 trillion per year, increased government regulation and mandates including federal healthcare coming shortly, *The Certainty Factor* is increasingly negative, which not only makes it difficult to try and keep employees (like Sally), but it virtually eliminates the prospects for committing company funds to hiring new workers, given the huge financial burden to the firm's cost structure. In the next chapter we'll examine the ripple effect that can be triggered from primary job creation, and how the additional concentric circles of new jobs flow from the initial business decision to hire a new worker.

JOB CREATION

Chapter 7

Secondary Job Creation: The Ripple Effect

Keeping taxes low and restraining spending leads to a vibrant economy and new jobs, better opportunities and a shrinking deficit.

- Former President
George W. Bush

The most basic complement to primary job creation is the ripple effect of the subsequent additional jobs. This secondary job creation is directly related to the economic impacts initiated by those initial hiring activities. When a company hires a new employee that action sets in motion a series of interconnected economic activities that include the hiring of other individuals across of a wide variety of independent and affiliated businesses. These include products and services linked to the infrastructure and operating plans tied to the first person hired in the process. A virtual chain reaction of interrelated distributing, supply, manufacturing, service and support, technical, and sales jobs have their genesis at that initial new job. Each subsequent hiring in this manner can trace its origin to one or more workers added at the center of the concentric circles of secondary job creation. Primary job creation acts like a hub of employment activity within a given market segment, sector, or industry. The pace of the ripple effect

JOB CREATION

ultimately depends on the level of aggregate optimism or pessimism for *The Certainty Factor* among all firms that comprise these various concentric layers around the primary position.

The U.S. economy is actually composed of thousands of these employment hubs. On the one hand, secondary job creation can happen going back up the value chain toward the suppliers of the raw materials, goods in process, and component parts. But it can also happen going forward, further down the value chain toward through the various wholesale and retail sales and distribution channels culminating with the ultimate end-users. Our focus is to demonstrate that job creation based on a strong *Certainty Factor* can easily become contagious throughout multiple levels of the economy. At the macro level, entire industries can get new employment kick started based upon significant positive job movement from one of the market leaders, or a rapidly adopted innovation. At the micro level, a few new people hired at one firm can also initiate more new jobs within the closer proximity of suppliers and distributors closer in to the hub. First we'll examine the concept of an employment multiplier, and then define examples of close proximity job creation on these subsequent levels. We'll conclude this chapter looking at the role of *The Certainty Factor* in geometric secondary job creation.

The Employment Multiplier

Entrepreneurial creation of self-sustaining jobs inevitably helps to also create secondary jobs across a broad range of both independent and related businesses. In this way, primary job creation has a multiplier effect increasing wealth and opportunity for not only the company's primary employees, but also affiliated businesses that depend on such employed consumers for their success. It is really fascinating that these affiliated and dependent businesses can then become primary employers in their own right, creating jobs for firms that service the business itself or the needs of its employees and customers. One can imagine concentric

JOB CREATION

circles of job creation emanating out from each of these primary businesses and overlapping so as to further multiply the positive economic impact of self-sustaining entrepreneurial job creation.

For example, adding employees generally signals an increase in the employer's overall business prospects, benefitting its suppliers and contractors, while creating additional job opportunities in these affiliated companies. In addition, newly created jobs increase employment opportunities in the area immediately surrounding the primary employer's location. As the number of people employed in a given area grows, retail businesses in that space such as restaurants, hotels, transportation, entertainment, and parking lots all benefit and create new job opportunities of their own. If the primary employer a retail business that attracts consumers (what those in the real estate business call an "anchor tenant"), other retail businesses will move into close proximity so as to serve the related needs of the anchor tenant's customers, in turn creating additional jobs and retail opportunities. Adding salaried employees also benefits the firms that these employees frequent near their homes, such as grocers, clothing stores, gas stations, banks, dry cleaners, video stores, places to eat, and car dealerships. Of course, each of the individuals employed in these secondary positions becomes a primary employee in relation to their own business, to satisfy their needs or the needs of their employer, and this further expands the job creation dynamic. These additional jobs grow outwardly from the primary enterprise generating additional new jobs in concentric circles of wealth creation and economic prosperity.

One way to think of the multiplier effect is in times of positive economic news, expansion, and strong profits. A prime example of this involves the tourism industry. Along a given main boulevard at a destination city there are hotels, restaurants, music clubs, parking garages, museums, art galleries, and a wide variety of shopping. When the economy expands, one of the first "luxury" or discretionary purchases that individuals and households probably

JOB CREATION

add in is vacation travel. Even businesses may allow for more company-related trips for employees, for things like trade shows, product expos, new client development, and existing customer service calls. In this positive mode, the employment multiplier brings a positive impact, starting first with more hotel rooms being booked as trips are increased in duration and frequency. It might start with the hotel staff, as some part-time employees have their hours increased to full-time, while other positions need to be added. The support staff at the convention hall will also be increased due to more attendance at the various events. Some events may be added or expanded in size because of significantly more demand and attendees pre-registered. This then continues at the restaurants, the clubs, the garages, the cultural stops, and the whole range of shopping options. Positions get added or have their hours scaled increased. Related product and service orders are increased, inventories on-hand start to drop, and greater demand begins to drive the actions of dozens of interconnected firms and employees on the supply side of goods and services.

In addition, the commercial travel that precedes tourists and business people arriving at the destination will also experience increases in traffic directly related to the "travel" expansion. For example, during the first half of 2010, "Hawaii's unemployment rate was between 6.7% and 6.9% - though the rate varied from island to island. Tourism and visitors were expected to pick up through the summer and fall seasons, which [would then] likely have a positive impact on the Hawaii employment multiplier." (*Hawaii Unemployment Situation Improves Slightly*, The MAUI NEWS (May 22, 2010) http://www.mauinews.com/page/content.detail/id/531774.html?nav=8).

The first secondary hiring effect involves close-in related workers within the same business. These are referred to as proximate job creation. If more cooks, servers, and waiters are needed in the food service department of a large hotel, that probably means more housekeeping and clean-up crews, as well as doormen, valets, and front desk personnel will also be hired. The ripple effect continues out to the fitness center, the pool, landscaping, and building maintenance. With increased patronage, all the facilities in the resort get more use and require more staff to keep things clean and running smoothly. Similarly, there will be a need for more phone operators and reservation assistants, and this might also translate into additional hires in the marketing, promotions, and corporate accounts area. There are no government grants, special tax credits, or federal work-training programs to make the employment multiplier get going. As with chapter six, the new hire is a business decision, and it comes with some ratio of related new jobs created.

The proximate job creation then begins to approach a second close-in concentric circle of directly related new positions that interact with, and are dependent on, the in-house new hires needed to support the upturn in the business. As individuals are hired at certain companies, perhaps hundreds or thousands of miles away from Hawaii, business decisions are made to have staff attend a trade show or convention, while personal decisions are made to book that luxury vacation in the islands. As the airlines see more demand for flights, the hotels experience increased room reservations, and the restaurants have more dining patrons. The clubs, cultural venues, and shops begin to see larger crowds while the taxis, rental cars, parking garages, and gas stations all experience improving traffic. At every level of the infrastructure that defines that city, new workers are needed to serve guests, pick-up and drop-off visitors and tourists, stock shelves, handle inquiries, and keep the retail businesses open longer hours.

The employment multiplier has been carefully studied and quantified for dozens of industries and business sectors in the U.S. economy. It measures both how many new jobs typically follow certain primary job creation at the hub, and how long is the average lag time between initial hires and the subsequent hiring of these tangent employees. In 2003, the Economic Policy Institute

JOB CREATION

found evidence that the multiplier in the manufacturing industries was higher than elsewhere in the economy. Research found that 100 jobs in manufacturing [generally] supports 2.91 jobs elsewhere in the economy, compared to 1.54 jobs in business services and 1.08 jobs in retail trade. (Bivens, J. "Updated Employment Multipliers for the U.S. Economy - 2003," *Economic Policy Institute No. 268,* August 2003). While there is no guaranteed way to specifically know how many new jobs will follow certain primary hiring in a given market, nearly three decades of labor multiplier research have yielded consistent support for the overall phenomenon.

Proximate Job Creation

Proximate job creation always starts with the primary businesses' own employees. This includes not only the employees who create, manufacture, promote, distribute or sell the primary businesses' products or services but also the in- house attorneys, accountants, administrators and other professionals such business requires to maintain its operations. In addition, the business may rely upon outside suppliers or professional who provide materials and services the business requires. Close proximity job creation comes as a direct result of the primary businesses' needs. It happens close in to the initial firm's hiring and has clear, direct connections to the new workers just added. Simple examples include more customers deciding to spend discretionary funds on premium satellite television. As more new orders come in, the firm hires more installation technicians and customer service reps to handle inquiries and to schedule service calls. In time, the firm may have to add workers in the billing department, as well as in accounts receivable. More trucks or vans will be leased or financed, and additional space will probably be needed for increased inventory and storage. The general contractor who does warehouse upgrades gets called by the satellite television firm and secures that new building project; this leads to adding two new part-time day laborers and one full-time carpenter to the contractor's staff.

JOB CREATION

The fleet leasing department at a local auto dealership gets the new account for the installation and service vehicles. Two bookkeepers and one accountant get placed as temps-to-hire given the increased sales and billing. The commercial realtor gets a previously vacant space signed on to a new 24-month lease. If customer sign-ups remain strong, the owner or franchisee begins plans to open a new location 30 miles away to focus on housing in that local area. That results in either more support staff at the existing home office, or hiring a new team to staff the expansion office. More real estate is rented, more vehicles are needed, and more installers and customer service reps will need to be hired.

The proximate employment multiplier is not always linear. It might show a 25% increase in new customer accounts translates into 8 new employees, while a 35% increase requires 14 new workers. Worker productivity in each area of the business operations will yield different ratios of new workers per sales growth. As was previously discussed in chapter three, entrepreneurs, owners, and managers look at their capital and labor uses, supply and demand and wages in the local labor market, and ROI on new hires. In addition, gains in marginal productivity from new hires, and economies of scale that reduce the costs of doing business, also factor into employment multiplier. The core concept remains that adding new workers in one area of the business will generally require hiring more people in complementary functional areas elsewhere in the firm.

Sometimes the multiplier has been referenced in the context of negative impacts to employment, where certain regulations of legislated requirements imposed on one sector or industry, form the basis for a multiplier backlash in another market segment resulting in job losses tied directly or indirectly to that government activity. For example, Thomas Sowell, a Hoover Institute Fellow at Stanford correctly notes that in many cases, "Tariffs that save jobs in the steel industry mean higher steel

JOB CREATION

prices, which in turn means fewer sales of American steel products around the world and losses of far more jobs than are saved". For the purposes of this book, our focus is on the impact of *The Certainty Factor* to motivate private sector job creation. While trade-offs do exist, as in the case noted by Sowell, we adhere to the most common context and application of employment multipliers as they relate to subsequent job creation that happens as a direct result of primary new hiring activity within the private sector.

The quick service restaurant business is a good example of how close proximity job creation works. For purposes of this analysis, we will consider the restaurant a primary job creator. However, its customers almost certainly will come from surrounding businesses or housing communities and will have employers of their own. In the respect, virtually all businesses are inter-related and depend on the success of other businesses for their own success. However, we need to start somewhere and quick service restaurants are businesses which exist in almost any American community and are perhaps more familiar than any other American business.

A quick service restaurant will generally require a manager to run the operation, cooks, people who wait on its customers and counter people who take the orders and accept payment. These individuals will also perform related functions such as cleaning and basic maintenance. Normally, a quick service restaurant that operates during all three day-parts (breakfast, lunch and dinner) requires about 25 employees. However, such restaurant is responsible for far more jobs than its basic 25 employees. To begin with, the restaurant may require architects, planners, designers and a construction company to build the unit. If the restaurant itself does not build the unit, the landlord will nonetheless employ such individuals. The restaurant will also require equipment such as refrigeration units to store the food, cooking systems to prepare the food, point of sale computer

JOB CREATION

equipment and programs to take the orders, relate the correct information to the cooks and charge customers for their orders. It will also require signage designed and installed so that people know something about the restaurant and readily know where it is located. This will require businesses that design, manufacture, sell, service and deliver such equipment. After the entrepreneur builds the restaurant, it will need such individuals for periodic remodels so it can maintain its appearance and feel as a desirable place to eat. It will also need to periodically update its equipment and signage to maintain and improve the quality of its products, its service and appearance. Once operational, the restaurant will require a regular and reliable supply of quality food and paper products. The production and delivery of such products creates jobs for everyone from the farmers who plant the crops or raise the herds to the farm workers who harvest the crops or tend the herds to the processors who prepare the products for shipment and the drivers who deliver the products to the restaurant's door.

This supply chain process creates jobs in the agricultural sector, processing and manufacturing sectors as well as the distribution business. When it has a place within which to operate and products to sell the restaurant will need to promote or advertise its products. Such promotion and advertising will cover everything from the look of the restaurant's menu, the point of sale materials in its windows, the signs or banners outside the restaurant, newspaper ads, radio ads, television ads and digital promotions. Such activities may require an advertising agency, a media buying firm, and actors as well as companies in the television, radio, Internet, and print businesses. There will also be businesses that help with repairs and maintenance of the restaurants such as heating and air conditioning repairmen, landscapers, window washers, and people to slurry the parking lot. As such, even a business as simple and commonplace as a quick service restaurant employs numerous individuals across a broad range of sectors, professions and businesses both small and large. The numerous businesses and employees involved in this process owe their

JOB CREATION

continued success and their jobs to the success of the restaurant that is, in this example, the primary job creating business. The more restaurants a business operates, the greater impact it has on creating these direct proximity jobs, and the more impactful it is generating jobs not only in the restaurant itself but in the concentric circles of job creation that emanate from the restaurant itself. This employment multiplier is an axiom of private enterprise, even though it is measured across a wide range of ratios, depending on the size and type of industry or market being analyzed. Entrepreneurs, business owners, and senior management at large corporations all understand the clear realities of this ripple effect, and the complementary nature of related new hiring. But that is what makes this concept not only fascinating, but also why it should be a prime driver of national job creation policies. Real private sector jobs (not temporary government work projects) are always interrelated with other functional aspects of businesses. Big government needs to understand clearly how to support a vibrant private sector, providing individuals and firms with a strong *Certainty Factor* and positive future expectations.

The Geometric Certainty Factor

Extended-proximity job creation is job creation unrelated to the function of the primary business itself. These new jobs happen much further out from the original hiring hub, and are not the complementary positions needed within the firm. This category of job creation includes a wide cross section of the broader macro-economy. Each of these will become its own hub and no doubt include proximate job creation of its own, there within its unique setting. But the lines can still be traced from firm to firm, industry to industry, and market segment to market segment, linking the original hiring function to what eventually ripples out to extended proximities well outside the close in range of the firm that started the employment ball rolling. The picture in your mind should first

JOB CREATION

see the original firm as a circle, and inside that area are several categories of workers by departments or functional areas of expertise. Proximate job creation starts within that hub, and both widens the circle as more workers are hired, while also showing two to three layers of concentric circles representing other new jobs directly tangent to the primary job creation source.

Now, expand this picture and notice that there are several of these very similar circles, each depicting a separate business that is hiring and expanding its internal job roster with both a larger circle and a few layers of concentric, direct-effect tangent jobs. In each case, these stand alone as "pockets of job creation" and are generally considered micro-economic phenomena, with more of an intra-firm profile of new hiring. But, as your mind's eye steps back further from this image, you begin to notice there are various lines connecting these hubs. Some of the lines go from circle to circle. Some connect the heart of the circle to another firm's concentric layers. And others are linking concentric layers at one hub to layers at another company's hub. This presentation resembles the map in the back of all commercial airlines' in-flight magazines, where they show all the cities they fly to and every one of the connections they service throughout their national or global network. In a few places there are fat hubs bursting with connecting lines, while other cities have fewer such interconnectivity within the flight scheme. That is an effective way to visualize extended proximity job creation, and that multiplicative transaction over time forms the basis for what we term *The Geometric Certainty Factor.*

While there are levels of job creation for the close-in proximity at and around each firm that's hiring, there are now broader economic *macro* ripples that extend inter-market, inter-segment, and inter-industry. And, each of these proximate hubs is in some way initiating related job creation within itself, close by around itself, and to varying degrees, further out into its extended

JOB CREATION

community of the private sector. This clearly means that job creation functions at a geometric level, and not on some fixed linear trajectory. So many layers of concentric circles and interconnectivity comprise a geometric rate of job creation, that might start slowly in a relatively few hubs, but can then take off quite rapidly as the overall economy experiences hundreds, thousands, and even millions of these ripples on the employment front. It's at this stage that the private sector demonstrates its true resiliency and wonder (yes, wonder). Jobs don't get parceled out one at a time in measured bureaucratic increments of government rationing through temporary spending programs. Instead, all over the private sector landscape, entrepreneurs, business owners, and senior managers are simultaneously starting the hiring process and triggering the hiring process in others through their own ripple effects.

It's at this geometric level of growth that the *invisible hand* shows itself again, and financial news print, television, and web media outlets report in amazement how "*the market added some 350,000 new jobs in the most recent month, bringing the total for the fiscal quarter to over 1.1 million workers now hired*". That is the beauty and elegance of the private sector's functionality when it is unhindered, without the burdens of oppressive taxation and government regulations, and the pervasive uncertainty it generates among individuals, households, and companies, causing them to delay or withdraw plans for spending, borrowing, investing, and adding new jobs to the U.S. employment tally. Returning to our previous quick service restaurant example, the individuals the restaurant itself employs will spend the monies they earn on items such as food, clothing, housing, medical care, educations and entertainment. The individuals the related concentric circle businesses employ (farmers, manufacturers, distributors, service providers, etc.) will similarly spend the monies they earn on both discretionary and non-discretionary items. This economic activity will create further concentric circle jobs beyond those the business itself directly created such as

JOB CREATION

grocery stores, malls, car dealerships, movie theatre, insurance companies, banks, and medical complexes. In turn, each of these businesses will create jobs and wealth for their employees. In this respect, government agencies, which receive their funding almost exclusively from tax revenues, do create extended proximity jobs and are part of the concentric circles of job creation. Job creation is job creation. The person holding a government job or a job in a business that supplies or services a government agency is just as employed as the person working in a restaurant. However, the problem with government job creation is that ultimately it cannot exist absent the tax revenues primary private sector jobs generate or government borrowings that are based on the prospect of future private sector generated taxes.

As noted above, government agencies and employees are tax consumers. Their incomes are dependent on tax revenues or the prospect of tax revenues. Such employees do pay a portion of their incomes back to the government in the form of taxes, as do most private sector employees. As socialist economies have historically and consistently demonstrated, it is absurd to assume that a government spending its tax revenue, which is only a portion of the workforce's total income, can then generate long term financial vitality by creating or recreating the very jobs that generate that total income and the associated tax revenue. A portion cannot recreate the whole when the underlying system lacks the entrepreneurial profit-driven dynamics that result in organic job and wealth creation. Generating vigorous economic growth and a job-creating environment based on tax dollars alone would be comparable to feeding 5,000 people with the loaves and fishes intended as lunch for one young boy. It happened once. But the odds of a repeat are comparable to the odds that an economically activist government could create a vibrant economy. This kind of government intervention always leads to considerable negative impact on *The Certainty Factor*. Conversely, rapid geometric job growth stemming from thousands of interconnected hubs of primary job creation is the result of strong positive

JOB CREATION

expectations for future economic prosperity, and that prosperity only happens when government has stepped back and away from trying to be the center of the American enterprise system. But we propose that it remains quite hard for socialist-activist politicians to excuse themselves to the sidelines of the private sector, because their mindset is fundamentally anti-capitalism, and they derive their sense of power and security from believing they are absolutely needed at the central planning hubs in Washington and the state capitols to plan, guide, direct, and monitor the economy toward their egalitarian objective. To compensate for their inability to generate economic vitality through spending current tax revenues alone, socialist governments engage in deficit spending, but even these borrowings are based on the lenders' belief that the prospect of future tax revenues from the private sector is sufficient to justify lending now.

The ultimate result is financial collapse, demonstrated by the former Soviet Union and the current experiments in Greece, Spain, Portugal, and Great Britain, which seem intent on exacerbating their current problems with even more government borrowing and spending. Their solution should simply be to emulate the most successful economy in the history of the world (the U.S.) and implement a merit based free enterprise system with government involvement limited to *facilitating* free enterprise and regulating any efforts to make it less free. Assuming political stability, the *Geometric Certainty Factor* drives profit driven close proximity and extended proximity job creation. The accompanying dynamic concentric circle wealth creation across broad sectors of the economy should be sufficient to resolve any nation's underlying economic woes. The historical success of the United States and the growing success of China would seem to make such an approach almost axiomatic. This makes the current push for increased government involvement in both job creation and the entire U.S. economy even more perplexing and troubling.

Chapter 8

Great Examples Politicians Can't Understand

"The first lesson of economics is scarcity. There is never enough of anything to satisfy all those who want it. The first lesson of politics is to disregard the first lesson of economics."

- Thomas Sowell,
Economist

Perhaps the most fundamental tenet of American private enterprise is that firms compete with one another to produce products and services for a given market. Those that have the better products or services, or the best prices (or both) are successful, while those that have poorer quality or less features and/or higher prices are unsuccessful. That's how competition works, that's how markets function, and that's what impacts consumer behavior and choice. Companies use pricing to find the balance between their supply and the market's demand. And within that price, there must be room to cover all the direct labor and materials costs associated with one unit of a good or service provided, as well as a gross profit on each sale made. That gross profit on each unit sold is then designated to the fixed overhead expenses of the enterprise. Once enough volume has been sold to

JOB CREATION

cover all the overhead, a pre-tax operating profit is made. Companies hone and perfect their own unique business models to delineate those three components:

1) How much they charge their buyers,
2) All the direct labor and materials costs of each sale, and
3) The overhead expenses for total operations.

If the product is sold for $300 to wholesale distributors, the direct labor and materials are $100 per unit produced, and the firm operates with $2 million in fixed expenses, the gross profit on every unit sold is $200 and the firm must do 10,000 units of volume to cover its overhead ($2 million divided by $200 gross profit per units sold). Every unit of volume beyond 10,000 contributes $200 per sale to the company's pre-tax operating income. The concept of this business model is very succinct. Sell less than 10,000 units and show an operating loss. Sell exactly 10,000 units and break even with all costs. Sell more than 10,000 units and show and operating profit.

Business Models and Job Creation

The business model is the metric that entrepreneurs, business owners, and senior managers must consult whenever job creation is considered. If the firm has positive expectations for strong growth of demand in the future, it can hire additional direct labor and/or administrative and support personnel. The wages paid to direct labor show up in the per unit costs of production. The wages and salaries paid to the other personnel show up in the fixed overhead expenses. If the new direct costs added to production bring increased productivity and economies of scale, the increased gross profit on each sale means adding new jobs ROI improves the company's initial ROI on each sale. While new fixed wages and salaries to the new administrative personnel increase overhead, the larger gross profit on each unit produced plus the

JOB CREATION

increased sales volume should together improve pre-tax operating income, and the overall ROI. That's a good business decision to create new jobs because it makes sense within the business model.

Back in chapter three, we examined how the private sector defines job creation, and how it is fundamentally a business decision to hire new workers. The entirety of the U.S. economy functions on a wide range or versions of business models – each one is unique in some manner to every company's individual products, services, labor pool, operating plan, market structure, plant and equipment, distribution channels, and sales plan. The ultimate question for any entrepreneur or business owner is then simply: *"If I hire new workers, will I make a strong profit on the increased commerce I expect to do?"* It seems an easy enough concept, that there should be a profit that remains after I subtract total expenses from total revenues. While accountants have devised complex formulas for determining how best to calculate profitability, in the end, the most important factor in the survival of any business is how much profit is left after all the bills are paid. This profit incentive is one of the core tenets of capitalism and American private enterprise. Profitability drives the private sector's business models, and determines how a business can grow over time, and how much internal capital will be available for investment in things like new equipment, R+D, new facilities, updated systems of operations, and new technologies – and ultimately investment in a larger workforce. In the final analysis, profits provide the basis for expansion, and without profits, there cannot be sustained growth and meaningful job creation. The genesis of the business model is that goods or services can be provided to a market at a cost that is less than what the buyers are willing to pay. That gap, or profit margin, creates a new funding source for modernizing and expanding operations, but it also builds wealth for the owners over time, and for employees. That wealth gets reinvested back into the economy in the form of both debt and equity capital provided to other businesses, who also modernize and expand, and hire more workers.

JOB CREATION

Having a robust profit margin is not a bad thing; in fact it's a very good thing. The buyers are already comfortable with the price they pay for the goods or services provided, so if the business can manage to keep its costs under that price, there is no malice in "profiting" from the buyers' decision to purchase what is offered at a price. This can easily be applied to any example in any market. I could make my own shirts from thread that I spin myself, from cotton that I grow and harvest myself. But if someone else can deliver to me a good quality well-made shirt for $18, I simply have to decide whether that's a fair price compared to what I actually get, and what my alternatives are if I don't buy that shirt. If the $18 is a competitive price for the finished shirt, why should the buyer be concerned that the apparel company made a profit?

It's the same with our painting, lawn mowing, and shoe shine businesses we had in our younger days. Any homeowner was free to paint her own house, but if someone else could do it for a price that is agreed as competitive and fair for the final product delivered (compared to all the time and effort of doing it one's self), why should the homeowner be upset that the painter made a profit on the work completed? If paying to have one's lawn mowed saves time and energy, the homeowner is happy with the final look of the yard, the agreed price was deemed fair and reasonable for that result, so if the young kid who mowed the lawn profits from that hard work, why should the homeowner care if he made a profit or not? If agreeing to a price charged by a boy at the commuter rail train stop, for him to shine your shoes right there on the platform, results in the boy making a profit on his time and costs for the can of polish, that's private enterprise at its best. If I buy a car for $20,000 and the auto manufacturer makes $3,500 should I be upset and somehow expect the car should have been sold to me for $16,500? It's the same for the $189 price for one night at a 4-star hotel, the $829 for a round-trip airfare to France, and $4.69 for a great burger at Carl's Jr. – if the buyer accepts the price as commensurate with the good or service provided, why

JOB CREATION

care that the business made a profit on the purchase? Business model profits create new jobs.

But far too often, most politicians cannot grasp why firms make profits, or more accurately, *should be allowed to make profits*. Government states, *"Why do you need profit?"* and incorrectly believes that such profits are sitting, neatly stacked on a back table, collecting dust just off the boardroom at the firm's headquarters. They also posit that some form of exploitation took place for the company to profit on the purchases made by the buyers. President Obama has often spoken very negatively about companies making "excessive profits". (For example, his April 2010 speech at Cooper-Union where he stated that "a free market was never meant to be a free license to take whatever you can get, however you can get it". (*Obama's Cooper Union Speech*, Capitol Confidential (April 22, 2010) http://blog.timesunion.com/capitol/archives/25311/obamas-cooper-union-speech/). Or his proposed windfall profits tax on the oil and gas industry to pay for his stimulus. (L. Chapman, *Obama Windfall Profits Tax on Oil and Gas Industry Could Fund Stimulus Plan*, The Huffington Post, (January 15, 2009) http://www.huffingtonpost.com/lloyd-chapman/obama-windfall-profits-ta_b_158172.html; *see also* Andrew Ferguson, *Obama's Crusade Against Profits*, THE WEEKLY STANDARD (June 26, 2010) http://www.weeklystandard.com/articles/obama%E2%80%99s-crusade-against-profits)). There is no basis for this, nor can he provide a clear definition of what constitutes *"excessive".*

His perspective is entirely subjective and a function of his own bias against private sector capitalism. He, like most politicians, has never started, operated, and grown a business. Their only personal financial experience is picking up their taxpayer-funded paychecks. Their other financial experience is raising taxes on hard-working individuals and businesses in the private sector, and spending that (plus additional borrowed funds) on regulations

JOB CREATION

and programs they control. But the irony is that private sector business models need strong profit incentives to spur growth plans and job creation at firms all across the country. While strong corporate profits "nurture a robust economy and job growth . . . [Obama] has nothing but disdain for the record profits of the insurance companies." (Barnes, Fred, *Know-Nothing-in-Chief*, THE WEEKLY STANDARD (August 3, 2009) http://www.weeklystandard.com/Content/Public/Articles/000/000/016/765kishz.asp). With no profit-based business models, private enterprise would not happen, and commercial transactions would function in backward Marxist-Leninist form, where the central government decides who gets what goods and services, who produces them and how many are produced, and how one uniform price is charged with no competition. We already know for certain that such a system can only lead to national economic failure.

All of private enterprise functions on some kind of business model. Regardless of the product or service produced, the industry, the competition, and the business model are comprised of the same basic components. Guess what? Apple's cost to produce and ship an iPod or iPad is actually less than what buyers pay for them, so Apple makes a profit on each unit sold. That profit goes to cover all the overhead of the Apple infrastructure, funds R+D for continued product innovations, provides capital for investing in Apple's growth, and allows the company to hire more people while opening more locations. Boeing's cost to build and deliver a commercial jet to United Airlines is actually less than what United pays for the aircraft, so Boeing makes a profit on each unit sold. Boeing pays dividends to shareholders, reinvests in plant and equipment, funds R+D on future product innovations. Sears also charges more for Kenmore washer-dryer combos than it costs to produce these. Gap charges more for Levis jeans than the Levi Strauss Company spends on labor and materials to produce each pair. Motorola sells its phones at prices above its costs of production, and makes a gross profit on each unit sold. The same holds true for 3-ring binders sold at Office Max, sneakers sold at

JOB CREATION

Sport Chalet, Harley-Davidson 1200cc cruisers, a gallon of Behr paint sold at The Home Depot, and Andy Puzder assures our readers, that a Carl's Jr. bacon guacamole burger is priced above CKE's direct costs of labor and materials to deliver that hot and juicy sandwich at any of its 3,100+ locations. If any of these products or services was incorrectly priced too high in its respective market, demand would drop and the company would no longer be a viable competitor. But they all seemed to be priced very well, because that business model accomplishes both: 1) Bringing in customers and 2) making a profit on each sale.

Andy's Billion Dollar Corporate Model

The ultimate question for me as President and CEO is: Are we making a profit? In other words, what remains after subtracting total expenses from total revenue? While accountants have devised complex formulas for determining how best to calculate profitability, in the end, the most important factor in the survival of any business is simply how much cash you have left after you pay all your bills. What remains are the cash profits produced, and they determine whether you grow the firm, change your business, or go out of business. In the final analysis, nothing else matters. With cash profits you survive and grow. Without them, you fail.

The profit model in the restaurants industry is fairly straightforward. At the restaurant level, we take total revenue and subtract our food costs, paper costs (wraps, napkins, etc), labor costs, occupancy costs (rent, repairs and maintenance, utilities, etc.) and the cost of advertising. What remains we call our restaurant level operating profit or margin. Beyond these direct "in the restaurant" expenses, there are also outside or "above the restaurant" expenses such as general and administrative expense. This expense includes salaries of individuals who support the restaurants but don't work in them (the CEO, the finance and accounting department, the legal department, human resources,

JOB CREATION

etc.), rent for the corporate headquarters, outside legal and accounting expense, interest expense on debt, and other similar above the restaurant expenses.

There are also certain non-cash expenses that are relevant for accounting and tax purposes. The best example of such an expense is depreciation. This is an expense which accountants use to recognize that hard assets like buildings and equipment become less valuable over time. Such assets normally appear on the books of a company at their cost when purchased plus any monies spent improving them. The accounting rules and tax laws then require or permit companies to reduce the book value of these assets by reducing their value over time. This reduction is called depreciation and it reduces not only the value of the assets on a company's books but also reduces that company's profits for accounting and tax purposes. It is a non-cash expense because, while it reduces profits, the business still has the cash. It is not an expense you actually pay. In fact, depreciation may reduce your tax liability and thereby actually increase your cash profits. As such, while depreciation will reduce the company's reportable profits, it is not an expense the company actually pays so the business may have more cash than it has profits.

The end result of this process of offsetting revenues and expenses is the business's pre-tax income or pre-tax profits. This is where the government steps in and reduces the company's profits through taxes. Taking the business's profits plus its non-cash expenses minus any taxes it has to pay basically results in its cash profits. This is what we refer to as the business's cash flow. It is what the entrepreneur can put in the bank at the end of the day. On the way to creating the firm's cash flow, the restaurant entrepreneur creates jobs across a broad spectrum of affiliated sectors. For example, the restaurant level expenses mentioned above may reduce profits, but they also represent the most direct ways in which restaurant companies create jobs.

JOB CREATION

Our company is known as CKE Restaurants, Inc. We own the Carl's Jr. and Hardee's brands. While not the largest fast food company (we are the fifth largest fast food hamburger company based on the number of restaurants behind McDonalds, Burger King, Wendy's and Sonic), we do own or franchise about 3,146 restaurants. We have restaurants in 42 states and 16 foreign countries. Entrepreneurs Carl Karcher, an Ohio native with an 8th grade education, and his wife Margaret, a California native, started the firm in 1941 with a hot dog cart in South Central Los Angeles. Our 200+ franchisees are also individual entrepreneurs who own and operate restaurants under the Carl's Jr. and Hardee's brands pursuant to franchise agreements with the Company. We own and operate 898 of our 3,146 restaurants. Our franchisees own and operate the remaining 2,248 restaurants or about 70% of our total restaurants. CKE currently employs about 23,000 people in the United States. Our domestic franchisees employ approximately an additional 49,000 people in the United States. As such, domestically we jointly account for about 72,000 jobs.

By operating our businesses, both the company and our franchisees generate job creation on a very broad scale. Looking at our restaurant level operating expenses and how those expenses generate direct and concentric circle jobs, in fiscal year 2010 (essentially calendar year 2009), our Company spent $312 million on restaurant level labor directly employing about 23,000 people in our domestic restaurants. Our franchisees employ an additional 49,000 people domestically, more than doubling what we spend on restaurant level labor. Moving to concentric circle jobs, our domestic food and paper expense was approximately $1 billion (Company and franchise restaurant purchases combined) creating jobs in the agricultural, manufacturing and distribution sectors. In essence, these monies go to create jobs for everyone from the farmers and ranchers who plants the seeds and tend the herds to the truck drivers who deliver the finished products to our restaurants. We also spent $33 million on restaurant repairs and

JOB CREATION

maintenance. This would include amounts we pay to small businesses for projects such as landscaping, air conditioning repair, window cleaning, and asphalt and parking lot repairs. As the franchisees own 70% of our restaurants, their repair and maintenance expenses are significantly in excess of the $33 million we spend. We also spent millions of dollars on media advertising for television, radio, newspapers, and other media outlets nationally. In 2009 alone, we spent $117 million (Company and franchise combined). All of these expenditures created jobs across a broad spectrum of our economy. In addition, there are the jobs created in businesses such as the grocery stores, clothing stores, gas stations, real estate agencies, doctors' offices and car dealerships that our employees and the employees of the affiliated companies we support utilize in their daily lives.

Having consistently created jobs with our restaurant level expenses including but going well beyond our 23,000 direct hires (or the 72,000 direct hires we have jointly with our franchisees), we also utilize the cash flow our business generates to further grow our business creating additional direct and concentric circle jobs. Businesses utilize their cash flow in different ways. The three principal ways we utilize our cash flow are: 1) reinvest the cash in our business to grow or maintain the business, 2) pay down debt, and/or 3) pay a portion to our shareholders through dividends. For fiscal year 2010, we generated cash profits of approximately $143 million. We reinvested the bulk of our cash flow back into remodels and building new units ($102 million). We paid a small dividend to our shareholders ($13 million), thereby returning a portion of our success to the people who own the Company. With the remainder of our cash profits, we paid down our debt by $28 million, which lowered our interest expense for the coming year and reduced the financial risk to our Company from any slowdown in business or increase in interest rates.

JOB CREATION

For job creation purposes, reinvesting is our business is our most important use of cash flow as debt repayment and dividends may strengthen the business and reward the owners but have little immediate impact on job creation. In the restaurant business, we principally create new jobs by building new restaurants. Every Carl's Jr. or Hardee's we build creates about 25 new direct hires in each new restaurant. New restaurant construction also creates jobs for numerous individuals and companies involved in the construction process including architects and designers, equipment and materials manufacturers and suppliers as well as the construction workers who build the new restaurants. As we increase the number of our restaurants, we not only create jobs with our direct labor costs and construction costs but we also increase the amount of food and paper products we purchase, the advertising we run and the amounts we pay to the small businesses that help maintain our restaurants. This growth in the number of restaurants we operate expands concentric circle jobs creation throughout a wide range of affiliated businesses and economic sectors.

Utilizing our cash flow to upgrade and remodel our restaurants also enables us to maintain the jobs we have already created and create new jobs for the designers who plan the remodels, the individuals who obtain the governmental approvals for the projects, the equipment and materials manufacturers and suppliers, and construction workers who complete such restaurant remodels. All this direct and concentric circle job creation based on our new unit and remodeling activity is dependent on the reinvestment in our business of its internally generated self-sustaining cash flow. Last year alone, this investment totaled $102 million or 71% of our total cash profits. Our business plan is simply to have cash at the end of the day that is in excess of our expenses and that allows us to reinvest in our business and continue to grow it. This growth results in increased profits further enhancing our growth potential. In essence, a profitably run firm generates cash flow, cash flow generate growth

JOB CREATION

and growth generates both direct and concentric circle job creation with a multiplier effect so extensive that is difficult to fully measure. In this respect, private enterprise is the driver of economic growth and job creation.

The notion that governments can tax businesses without negatively impacting economic growth is based on the mistaken notion often held by those within government that the phrase "business profits" is synonymous with the term "excess cash" (the "corporate pot of gold" theory). As such, governments seem to believe that they can absorb this "excess cash", expend it on government projects and programs lacking either a profit motive or a growth incentive, without a meaningful impact on job creation and economic growth. When politicians propose new projects or programs, the assumption appears to be that firms can simply go to the corporate closet and dip into the "corporate pot of gold" for the monies needed to fund the proposed project or program without any damage to the company's business or ability to remain profitable and continue to grow and create jobs. While there are certainly limited examples of companies and businesses that have horded, squandered and misused their profits, the majority of businesses are run on the basis that they need to grow to survive and that cash flow is a prerequisite to growth. You cannot grow absent cash to invest in your business. There are two ways to get such cash: You can either borrow it (and pay interest on the loan) or you can generate it. Businesses have very little incentive to hold onto the cash they generate. Holding on to cash you generate is simply bad business. Cash is a depreciating asset. In other words, it goes down in value as you hold it. This loss of value is principally due to inflation that inherently devalues cash. As such, there is very little incentive for entrepreneurs or corporations that run profitable businesses to horde their cash.

The only rational thing for an entrepreneur or a business to do is to invest their cash where it will get the best ROI. Generally

JOB CREATION

speaking, you get the best return on your money from re-investing in your businesses. If you can get better returns in another business, you should invest in that business and get out of the one you are in. Entrepreneurs reinvesting in their businesses provide the fuel for economic growth and job creation. Cutting off an entrepreneur's ability to invest in his business by redirecting his cash flow to government programs and projects siphons off the funds necessary for growth and job creation and places those funds in the hands of entities and individuals who lack the incentive, the need or the ability to generate the profits required for self sustaining growth and meaningful job creation.

For example, the impact on our business model and job creation from the health insurance legislation will be devastating for our company's, and our industry's, ability to grow and create jobs. As already noted, last year we spent $102 million (71% of our free cash flow) on capital expenditures. Much of this was for items essential to the successful continuation of our business, including updating infrastructure, remodeling and repairing restaurants, (air conditioning or heating, roof repairs, bathrooms, parking), and updating our IT and distribution capabilities to stay competitive. We consider these expenses non-discretionary. On the discretionary side, we invested approximately $19 million in new restaurants which have, as discussed above, a very positive impact on job creation. Beginning in 2014, should we have to provide health insurance under the current law as we understand it and based on our current payroll, our health insurance expense would be approximately $23 million. This is the amount the company pays for health insurance. We currently pay approximately $12 million for health insurance. Assuming no increase to employee contribution amounts, this is an increase in health insurance costs for our company of over 90%. Our annual health insurance costs would equate to approximately 120% of our entire investment in new restaurants last year. The 90% increase in health insurance costs would cut our funds available

JOB CREATION

for growth by nearly 60%. It would similarly reduce our ability to create new jobs.

Our current plan is to build 56 restaurants over the next four years directly creating approximately 1,400 new jobs which will create far more concentric circle jobs for our suppliers and affiliated businesses. Our franchisees, who will also have to incur these health care costs under the proposed legislation, plan and have committed to build over 300 domestic restaurants over the next four years directly creating 7,500 new jobs, plus the associated concentric circle jobs for our suppliers and affiliated businesses. Faced with substantially increased health insurance costs, both our company and our franchisees will also have to substantially reduce new restaurant development and the associated job creation such new restaurant development generates.

With the unemployment rate higher than it has been in decades, our national focus needs to remain on job creation. What our elected officials must understand is that balancing our priorities does not involve a choice between government welfare programs like government health acre on the one hand, and corporations squandering or hording wealth on the other. The choice is between taxpayer funded welfare programs and dynamic economic growth with the associated job creation. This is a balance our lawmakers must perform with care lest they enervate or destroy the most successful wealth creation and distribution system in history and replace it with a government dominated system that has failed miserably everywhere and every time it has been tried. This directly affects *The Certainty Factor* for our company. When the risks from the federal government are greater than the risks from competitors, economic decline and sustained recession are inevitable. That is currently the case for much of the American business community. Perhaps out of a conscious choice, perhaps out of ignorance with respect to how economic growth and job creation actually work, government has become, and looks to *remain*, the enemy of growth.

JOB CREATION

Dave's Entrepreneurship Start-Up Model

Since 1984, I have consulted to more than 150 entrepreneurial start-ups and emerging growth ventures between San Diego and Silicon Valley, as well as in ten other states and Europe (Switzerland, Germany, Luxembourg, France, and England). While the products and services, and levels of innovation impact, vary from one company to another, the common facet of each firm is a viable, sustainable business model. Every successful entrepreneur understands that the product or service sells for a targeted price, and then generates a gross profit on each sale - net of the direct costs to produce/deliver that product or service. And the business must do a minimum level of sales activity in order to have enough gross profit to cover the new venture's fixed overhead costs (the *burn rate*). Venture capital groups, angel investors, private equity funding, and banks ALL look at the same basic metrics in order to determine the viability of the company and its long-term sustainability in the market. So while my co-author Andy's previous section covered the business model and job creation from the perspective of a billion dollar corporation, I will briefly examine the business model and job creation as they relate to entrepreneurial start-up and emerging growth ventures.

The reality is that, while the dollar values differ quite a lot between these two types of businesses, the core interactions of the business models and sustainable job creation remain exactly the same, and so should one's perspective of the business decision to hire new workers. This truth should hopefully have a huge impact on the thinking of politicians and other government bureaucrats who are often quick to laud American small business and tout their nominal support for helping "the little guy", but tend to have very negative views of American big business, based upon a few firms in the ultra-minority who happen to make front page headlines due to some kind of scandal, fraud, or corruption. In the end, small entrepreneurial growth firms and large established

JOB CREATION

national corporations both function with a clear business model aimed at making a profit and building wealth for the owners over time. A very simple example is that while a Carl's Jr. burger sells for $4 and contributes a gross profit margin to the multi-million dollar corporate overhead on each unit sold, a recently launched small gourmet restaurant sells specialty sliders for $4 - which also contributes a gross profit margin to the few hundred thousand dollars of annual overhead on each unit sold. Carl's Jr. makes its model work based upon volume. The start-up eatery makes its model work on a proportionate volume, even though it's just a tiny fraction of the former. And BOTH companies do job creation based upon the upside potential success of its business model.

In each of the ventures I have consulted to, the entrepreneur always explains to me the innovative approach and features of the new product or service. Having identified the target market and a plan to promote and advertise this innovation, the focus then turns to the business model and its relationship to growth prospects and employment needs. Just like Carl's Jr. (and Apple, Boeing, Sears, Gap, Motorola), the product will be priced above the direct labor and materials costs to produce a gross profit on each unit sold, and then a requisite volume must be sold to cover the venture's burn rate. The entire upside profit potential of the entrepreneurial enterprise rests on the viability of the business model to meet the targeted sales, costs, margins, and overhead of these forecasted metrics. Job creation for each emerging start-up company happens on two levels. First, the business model identifies how many hourly workers can be supported in the production or manufacturing area. Typically, the direct costs of labor are higher on a per unit basis when the firm is just getting launched, because there is not enough volume of output over which to spread those hourly wages, which increases the average labor cost per unit. Of course, this average labor cost will come down as output ramps-up to meet growth. Second, the business model identifies how many salaried workers can be supported in the fixed costs of management, administration, and support staff.

JOB CREATION

This burn rate can often appear high in the earliest stages of the launch, relative to the size of the company's sales. But as sales growth continues over time, the fixed burn rate will be proportionately smaller and smaller.

The entrepreneur's business decision to add any new hourly workers has to be weighed in light of the effect on the direct costs of production and the resulting gross profit per unit. Any plans the new venture team has to add more managers and other fixed pay employees is then compared to the incremental increase it brings to the overhead expenses, and how much additional sales volume will be needed to cover those new salaries. When our team sits down with the founding team, and opens up a spreadsheet file with the business model clearly formulated, it's a very easy management decision process to plug in more hourly wages or salaries, and then see the effect these will have on required sales volume, gross profits, and overall company profitability. When future prospects look sound and optimism about growth and expansion is strong, hiring more workers translates into excellent opportunities to build the customer base and increase profits. But when the future is not in clear focus, and pessimism weakens thoughts about growth and expansion, any plans to consider hiring more workers are diminished in value. Concerns about the economy due to high taxes, fees, compliance, inflation, and consumer confidence, hurt any opportunities for building the customer base and better profits.

The Certainty Factor and Business Models

It's a precarious position for an emerging company to want to add new jobs. Hourly wages will increase the direct costs of output and initially decrease the gross profit on each unit sold. Salaried employees will increase the overhead and require additional sales volume to cover those new fixed expenses. This clearly illustrates why *The Certainty Factor* is so crucial to how entrepreneurs,

JOB CREATION

owners, and managers assess their business models relative to private sector job creation. It's also equally a balancing act for large national corporations to hire new workers. Opening up a new facility or expanding production capacity at an existing plant may at first push direct labor costs much higher per unit of output, and lower the profit margin on each sale, while the company waits for the forecasted sales growth to actually happen. Adding several new salaried managers, administrators, and support personnel will also initially push overhead costs higher, even before the anticipated new sales volume is realized. When prospects for market growth and increased profits are crippled by excessive government regulations and higher taxes, this negatively affects *The Certainty Factor* and causes companies to scale back, postpone, or even cancel plans for hiring new employees. Taking on those extra direct costs hurts the profit margin, and any new overhead costs will reduce overall profitability. Even if there is some potential for increased sales, higher federal and state income taxes, continued federal and state deficit spending, new fees to meet more regulatory compliance, higher property taxes, and other legislated costs to meet things like mandated federal health care or related government agency requirements ALL greatly reduce certainty and diminish future expectations. Multiply these kinds of negative projections across tens of thousands of businesses, and millions of individuals and households, and new job creation is halted while many existing employees are laid off.

However, when prospects for the future look strong, due to scaled back government spending, less regulations, reduced paperwork and compliance, and lower taxes across-the-board, *The Certainty Factor* improves dramatically and fosters strong positive expectations about sales growth, profits, and building wealth over time. This is the perfect environment to kick-start the geometric job creation discussed in the previous chapter. Individuals and households have increased certainty about their employment status and regular monthly income, with more of their wages and salaries staying in their take-home pay rather than going to more

JOB CREATION

and more government withholding. Companies have increased certainty about their market positioning, the competition, pricing, cost structures, and opportunities for growth, so they begin to add new workers. Those newly employed workers further bolster the certainty of individuals and households. Consumer spending picks up, and firms also begin to make new purchases of capital goods and inventory. Banks have more funds on deposit and more money to lend.

That is the kind of robust economic private sector that will rapidly create jobs, dramatically reducing unemployment. The U.S. economy does not need the federal government to raise taxes and borrow trillions of dollars through Treasury bills, notes, and bonds, and then allocate those funds across politically motivated and manipulative spending programs in the hope of stimulating job creation. Do the math. If the $800 billion stimulus legislation had been just equally divided among the 25 million or so businesses in the U.S. that would only amount to a one-time grant of $32,000 per firm, and would never be remotely close to enough funds to uniformly initiate a recovery. "Stimulus packages and tax increases that fund [increased] government spending burdened our economy in the 1930s and significantly hurt Japan's economy in the 1990s; money cannot go into the economy without first coming OUT of it, by extracting through borrowing and taxation, which leads to mere redistribution. Japan spent $840 billion in stimulus packages to stimulate the economy in the 1990s, and instead ended with a load of debt, [and] the U.S. has neglected to learn from their mistakes." (Veronique de Rugy, *Why the Stimulus Won't Work*, REASON.COM (Feb. 13, 2009) www.Reason.com/archives/2009/02/13/why-the-stimulus-plan-wont-wor).

Business models work. They have always worked for companies in the private sector, and they will continue to guide and direct business decisions about spending, borrowing, saving, investing, and job creation. "[But] excessive government necessarily causes the misallocation of labor and capital, and the high tax rates needed to finance that level of government will discourage work, saving, and investment." (Daniel Mitchell, *Competitiveness Means Less Government, Not More*, THE HERITAGE FOUNDATION (April 20, 2006) http://www.heritage.org/research/reports/2006/04/competitiveness-means-less-government-not-more). In the next chapter, we'll propose a very straightforward plan to get the private sector back into the job creation mode. These initiatives will utilize everything we have covered in this book so far, recognizing that job creation is a business decision, made by and in the private sector, based upon value-added marginal productivity, economies of scale, and ROI impacts to each firm's business model, motivated by a strong *Certainty Factor,* with the optimism of future opportunities for growth in sales, profits, and building sustainable wealth for companies and employees.

JOB CREATION

Chapter 9

A Straightforward Plan for Job Creation

*"Government's view of the economy
can be summed up in a few short phrases:
If it moves, tax it. If it keeps moving, regulate it.
And if it stops moving, subsidize it."*

- President Ronald Reagan

Reagan's assessment of how politicians perceive the economy remains just as valid today as it was in the 1980s when he expressed his frustration with the Washington establishment he inherited. The current administration and the political establishment elites in state and federal legislatures are literally doing everything you would NOT want to do with regard to helping create jobs, building wealth, and providing more incentives and opportunities for businesses and individuals. Their policies and mindset line up contrary on every front to the principles of robust private sector business development and job creation. They do the exact opposite of what a common sense individual would easily recognize should be done to free creativity, innovation, optimism, and new enterprise. On the federal level, the Senate and the House of Representatives are supposed to provide a voice for all of the country's citizens to be heard in the various matters of governing this great nation. But far too often, those individuals charged with that solemn

JOB CREATION

responsibility have instead pursued a course of political self-preservation, focused instead as career politicians on keeping themselves in office and in places of power regarding legislative policies and finances. To further promote their personal agendas, they need government funds under their jurisdiction to distribute to programs and laws that they deem important to either their political careers or their elitist ideological agenda.

Yet, even the taxes the Internal Revenue Service collects are insufficient to cover all that spending. So, the politicians borrow additional funds through the U.S. Treasury to fill the deficit gap between their total federal budget and the revenue with which they are supposed to work. Then when something (a person or a business entity) is out in the economy moving, functioning, creating, performing, generating income and building wealth, government taxes that activity under the rubric that the citizenry has an obligation to share a portion of those funds with the government – supposedly so that relatively small proportionate shared taxes pooled from across all fifty states will collectively benefit the nation as a whole. When that same person or entity continues to move and function in a sustainable manner, government next steps in to impose its own ideals on the private party's actions, through laws and other regulatory requirements that it justifies as "necessary" to ensure that no one's freedom of activity gains at the expense of another's position or perspective. Finally, once the taxes and legal constraints are in place, they tend to stay in place and morph into new or increased taxes and regulations over time, as government expands its role and increases its power over the private sector.

We need a new direction for the economy and the government. We need a plan that is practical, straightforward, and makes common sense. We don't need overly complex and unworkable theoretical models about how to create jobs. The last one hundred years provide overwhelming empirical evidence that the private sector always has been, and always will be, the best creator of new

JOB CREATION

jobs, and the most efficient responder to new economic opportunities. Put money back in the hands of businesses and individuals and get government off to the sidelines and out of the way. The U.S. economy has proven to be very resilient in rebounding from a wide range of downturns. We need a strong *Certainty Factor* to spur positive expectations about spending, saving, investing, and hiring. We need to completely stop the government's expanded intrusion into the private sector through taxes and regulations that allow it to then subsidize the persons, firms, and markets it deems worthy. We need to completely rid ourselves of the government mindset that requires those individuals and firms who are sustainable and functioning to *ante up* even larger proportions of their income, profits, and wealth in order to artificially carry others. Ultimately, we must turn government away from penalizing the successful to compensate those who are not. Is it any wonder that politicians who know and understand only government look right past the *invisible hand* of the individuals and firms that naturally and logically have always filled the gaps in the economy through innovation and competition, and instead look to their own very *visible* hands to regulate and control economic activity with taxes, fees, regulations, tariffs, and other legislated requirements?

Lessons From Jeff Foxworthy's Fifth Graders

Comedian Jeff Foxworthy's provides a great analogy about how the private sector and government relate to one another. On his television show, "So You Think You're Smarter Than A Fifth Grader", he asks common sense general knowledge questions and the adults show great pains in trying to decide whether they know the answers or whether the fifth-grade kids have the correct common sense response. The relationship between politicians and free markets is very similar. Think of it as the fundamental Job Creation Algorithm (JCA). Any individual or business owner is asked about the economy and understands very easily that the JCA is not quantum physics, nuclear fission, or the proverbial "rocket-

JOB CREATION

science". It makes perfect sense that: 1) free markets - with ease of entry and exit – have always fostered opportunities to compete (with lower taxes and reduced regulations). So, 2) a wide range of short-term and long-term financial providers inject equity and credit for individuals and firms to engage in multiple levels of commercial activities. Then, 3) opportunities increase and markets further develop and expand. This results in 4) individuals and companies hiring more people to get the additional work done in a timely manner or, simply stated, job creation. The overwhelming majority of US citizens would readily agree that having a great idea and starting a new business is far and away one of the time-tested hallmarks of what it means to be free, and an American. It makes fifth-grader common sense that elected officials at city hall, the county seat, the state capitol, or inside the Beltway are incapable of legislating or mandating these opportunities. It makes fifth-grader common sense that: 1) the government taxes too many activities, 2) at rates that are too high, and 3) there are far too many government regulations, 4) and compliance requirements imposed on businesses and individuals.

Average common sense Americans know without a doubt that they are over-regulated and over-taxed, while their elected officials do nothing but spend and borrow in reckless excess. The politicians – who are supposedly wiser and more sophisticated in their knowledge of "how things work" and "what's best for the economy" (after all, they are Senators, House Representatives, Economic Advisors with PhDs, agency heads, White House counsels, press secretaries, community organizers, and even the President of our great nation) – actually look and sound ridiculous in their measured press conferences and staged photo-ops. They stand in their professional poses, fingers rubbing their chins and eyes squinting into nowhere, as they wax a sophisticated tone void of substance and without content or merit, that *they* truly know what's best. Why? Because they speak and act within a bureaucratic and academic bubble, isolated from the realities of daily American life in the private sector. Their *raison d'être* is all

JOB CREATION

about their own power, perspectives, and agendas for advancing their political careers, while mandating ideologically based and unaffordable social programs. They have never started a company, administered a payroll, been responsible to secure sales contracts, had to manage costs and balance budgets, produce a product or service, or show a profit to the shareholders. The common sense average American readily "gets it" – job creation would flourish if government would dramatically cut taxes, decrease regulations, and reduce runaway spending. That's the correct response about how to get job creation going again.

How can the political elites treat the JCA as if there is no clear evidence or track record of how our free market economy has consistently and dynamically created jobs for decades? Because they believe that government intervention on multiple levels is the only way to put people to work. Wrong answer! Elected officials attempt to legislate where growth should come from, who will experience it, how much is enough, what a worker should be paid, and how those challenged by new change and innovation can be cared for and compensated if their products and services have been supplanted by better and lower cost alternatives. Wrong solution! Any common sense fifth-grader would immediately concur, that "to reduce unemployment, the economy needs more private sector hiring; but unfortunately, the policies pursued by Congress and the [Obama] Administration actively discourage this solution." (Rea Hederman & James Sherk, *Heritage Employment Report: May Jobs Struggle to Appear*, HERITAGE FOUNDATION (June 4, 2010), http://www.heritage .org/research/reports/2010/06/heritage-employment-report-may-jobs-struggle-to-appear). For there to be robust job creation and economic prosperity, even politicians at this point should recognize that their priority should always be to support individuals and businesses, by reducing or removing restrictive taxes and regulations that cripple, and even eliminate, enterprising opportunities.

JOB CREATION

Government Must Stop Creating Fear and Uncertainty

To take advantage of *The Certainty Factor*, and release the dynamic job creation potential of our free enterprise system, the government's role is to create a stable business friendly environment. The business community views the initiatives that an administration pursues as indicative of its attitude towards business and its concern for economic growth. In the respect and at the very least, the current administration should avoid legislative initiatives such as Universal Health Care, Cap and Trade, and Card Check that create fear and uncertainty in the business community, discourage growth and investment and have a prolonged negative impact on the economy as a whole. Taken together, these initiatives represent a politically motivated agenda targeted at regulating the business community and restricting entrepreneurial activity so as to accomplish ideological and social objectives. They also indicate to the business community an anti-business mindset that has created broad reaching uncertainty stifling both economic growth and job creation. When entrepreneurs are unable to predict what government will do next to impede their efforts and, therefore, are unable to forecast with reasonable certainty the potential profitability of a venture, they will not invest, they will not grow and they will not create jobs.

An administration discourages economic growth when, for example, to advance an anti-business agenda the President of the United States repeatedly engages in politically motivated diatribe such as labeling business leaders as "fat cats," treating the Chamber of Commerce as a shill for foreigners trying to influence domestic policy, and criticizing the business community for "driving the economy into a ditch," while taking advantage of employees, consumers and borrowers (Ken Langone, *Stop Bashing Business, Mr. President*, WALL STREET JOURNAL (October 15, 2010), http://online.wsj.com/article/SB10001424052748704361504575552080488297188.html). The President does little to mollify the business community by then claiming with much

JOB CREATION

bravado that he is not "anti-business." (Brian Montopoli, *Obama: Don't Call Me Anti-Business*, CBSNEWS.COM (Sept. 20, 2010), http://www.cbsnews.com/8301-503544_162-20017009-503544.html). Unlike much of the electorate, the business community will judge this President not by what he says or the eloquence with which he says it but rather by the agenda he pursues and what he actually accomplishes. So far, neither his agenda nor his accomplishments have been in any way either encouraging or intended to create positive certainty in the business community.

Supposedly the most significant accomplishment of the Obama presidency has been the passage of ObamaCare, a 2,800-page bill that legislators failed to read and clearly failed to understand. In fact, it is a law that no one understands making it virtually impossible for employers to get professional guidance because there are no professionals who truly understand it. The Health and Human Services Department has already had to grant dozens of waivers to certain ObamaCare mandates so that certain employers (most prominently McDonalds) and insurers (Cigna and Aetna) could continue offering medical coverage. AT&T had to take a $1 billion charge due to the passage of ObamaCare. Caterpillar Inc., AK Steel Holding, 3M and many other firms have all recorded similar charges against earnings and this is before ObamaCare's major provisions even take effect (Ian King & Amy Thomson, *AT&T to Book $1 Billion Cost on Health-Care Reform (Update-3)*, BUSINESSWEEK.COM (March 26, 2010), http://www.businessweek.com/news/2010-03-26/at-t-to-take-1-billion-charge-on-health-care-reform-update1-.html). Despite Nancy Pelosi's famous comment that "[w]e have to pass the bill so you can find out what is in it," no one understands what is in this law and what the business community does understand, it dislikes. (David Freddoso, *Pelosi on Health Care: "We Have to Pass the Bill So You Can Find Out What's in It...."* WASHINGTON EXAMINER (March 9, 2010), www.washingtonexaminer.com/opinion/blogs/beltway-confidential/ Pelosi-We-have-to-pass-the-bill-so-you-can-find-out-whats-in-it-87151897.html). This uncertainty is inhibiting

JOB CREATION

investment and job creation as it is virtually impossible for entrepreneurs and businesses looking to expand their hiring to determine what going forward costs are going to be and, as such, what returns any business investments will generate. Under these circumstances, *The Certainty Factor* is all but non-existent.

Efforts to enact Cap and Trade measures have similarly contributed to a climate of business uncertainty. Cap and Trade measures are designed to set a cap or a limit on carbon dioxide emissions from the use of fossil fuels. The government would give each covered oil company, utility, transportation company and manufacturing facility allowances or caps based on a formula involving past emissions or other criteria. The trade part of Cap and Trade would allow companies that emit less carbon dioxide than the formula permits to sell the excess to those who emit more than the formula permits. The government would progressively lower the caps for all businesses over time forcing businesses to ration their use of coal, oil, and natural gas in the US.

While it is difficult to gauge the costs of legislation which has yet to pass, we do know that fossil fuels currently provide 85% of our energy. Imposing a transition to other economically non-viable energy sources would, at least in the short term, undoubtedly be very expensive and detrimental to economic growth. As stated in the Wall Street Journal: "The whole point of cap and trade is to hike the price of electricity and gas so that Americans will use less. These higher prices will show up not just in electricity bills or at the gas station but in every manufactured good, from food to cars. Consumers will cut back on spending, which in turn will cut back on production, which results in fewer jobs created or higher unemployment." (*The Cap and Tax Fiction*, WALL STREET JOURNAL (JUNE 26, 2009), http://online.wsj.com/article/SB124588 83756 0750781.html. *See also* Ben Lieberman, *Beware of Cap and Trade Climate Bills*, FREE REPUBLIC (December 6, 2007), http://www.freerepublic.com/focus/f-news/2194995/posts). The reality is that the cost of all manufacturing or the delivery of any product in

JOB CREATION

the US will increase should Congress pass and the President sign Cap and Trade legislation. Whether or not production of a given product requires fossil fuels, every product has to be delivered to a point of sale or use and whether by truck, train or plane, the means of delivery invariably require gas and oil.

Notably, the Congress that passed ObamaCare was unable to pass Cap and Trade legislation. One would assume that this failure by a Congress dominated by Democrats and guided by a President fully supportive of such measures would create some certainty that this costly and economically destructive legislation was behind us. Unfortunately, this is not the case. The Obama Administration intends to "press ahead unilaterally with proposals using the Environmental Protection Agency's (EPA) existing authority under the Clean Air Act." (John Kemp, *Obama Mulls Cap and Trade by Decree*, REUTERS (April 14, 2009), http://blogs.reuters.com/great-debate/2009/04/14/obama-mulls-cap-and-trade-by-decree/. See also, *The EPA Permitorium*, Wall Street Journal (November 22, 2010) http://online.wsj.com/article_email/SB10001424052748704658204575609241685198241-lMyQjAxMTAwMDIwMzEyNDMyWj.html). In other words, even without legislation, "[t]he Obama administration is considering a carbon-trading system under existing law if Congress doesn't pass cap-and-trade legislation that allows companies to buy and sell the right to pollute. . ." (Simon Lomax, *EPA Studying Own Carbon Trading System Official Says (Update2)*, BLOOMBERG (March 15, 2010), http://www.bloomberg. com/apps/news?pid=newsarchive&sid=ammjHfzRpc9I). According to Bloomberg, a senior policy analyst at the EPA , stated that "[t]he existing Clean Air Act 'could enable us to include emissions trading' within agency regulations aimed at reducing carbon dioxide and other gases that scientists have linked to climate change. . . . While the agency 'strongly prefers' that Congress pass new laws dealing with greenhouse gases, 'we think that there's a lot of progress that can be made using certain tools under the Clean Air Act.'" (*EPA Studying Own Carbon Trading System*, BLOOMBERG, March 15, 2010).

JOB CREATION

Whether by hook or crook or stretching the EPA's regulatory authority to the breaking point, this Administration intends to continue to push Cap and Trade measures. As with ObamaCare, the Administration's pursuit of Cap and Trade initiatives creates broad based uncertainty inhibiting investment and job creation. The impact such a measure would have on our economy is extremely difficult to predict beyond the very obvious prediction that it would be severe and detrimental. If you are looking to start a business in the US or expand an existing one, the specter of Cap and Trade looms large creating a lack of certainty discouraging both growth and job creation.

Card Check is another Obama administration agenda item that has businesses reconsidering whether to grow and looking to retrench. Under the measures Congress has considered since President Obama took office, the Card Check process would replace the secret ballot election currently required before an employer has to recognize a union. This process would compel employers to recognize a union as soon as the union acquired a majority of signed cards from employees stating a desire to unionize. Unfortunately, Card Check would eliminate the anonymity and privacy of the current federally supervised secret ballot election process, and, as such, lend itself to intimidation and coercion in the organizing process. To avoid such intimidation and coercion is why Congress created the federally supervised secret ballot election process in the first place. Card Check would allow unions to eliminate secret ballots, broadly considered a basic American right, and unionize companies simply by cajoling, intimidating or coercing a majority of workers into signing a card. (*The Employee Free Choice Act—The 'Card Check' Bill*, USCHAMBER.COM, http://www.uschamber.com/issues/labor/employee-free-choice-act-card-check-bill).

In addition to depriving workers of the right to vote by secret ballot, the version of Card Check that was most recently before Congress (ironically called "The Employee Free Choice Act") also would have required binding arbitration if management and labor were unable to reach a collective bargaining agreement once a union was certified under the card check process. If the employer and the union were unable to reach agreement within 120 days the Card Check law would force them into binding arbitration. In other words, a panel of government arbitrators lacking any understanding of the employer's business could impose a two year contract with all workplace terms on that employer. Most prominently, such workplace terms would include the cost of labor, a major expense in any business and one any reasonable entrepreneur would want to understand thoroughly before starting a business or expanding an existing employee base. (*The Employee Free Choice Act—The 'Card Check' Bill,* USCHAMBER.COM).

As the no longer existent American garment industry or segments of the increasingly non-competitive American automotive industry well demonstrate, empowering unions can increase labor costs to the point of putting employers in or near bankruptcy. This is in best interests of the neither employees, employers nor our potential for economic growth. One need only compare the growth of the automotive industry in Michigan (a state with favorable union organizing laws) to that in Texas and Mississippi (right-to-work states where employees cannot be compelled to join a union as a condition of employment). As such, Entrepreneurs looking to start a business or employers looking to add employees will be less inclined to do so under the specter of potential and increasingly likely unionization. The specter of Card Check again creates an uncertain economic environment making it difficult to forecast the potential profitability of any given business and thereby discouraging investment, growth and job creation.

While Card Check is another Obama agenda item that failed to get through a Congress dominated by Democrats, like Cap and Trade, the Obama administration is not giving up. In March 2010, unable to get Senate *Democrats* to approve the appointment of labor lawyer Craig Becker to the National Labor Relations Board

(NLRB), President Obama gave him a recess appointment to this Board to oversee union elections. "As a top lawyer for the Service Employees International Union, Mr. Becker had suggested that the NLRB has the legal authority to impose card check—which eliminates secret ballots in union elections—without the approval of Congress. At the end of August the NLRB dropped the bombshell, when, in a 3-2 decision, it decided to revisit its important 2007 *Dana Corp.* ruling." (*Back Door Card Check*, WALL STREET JOURNAL (September 14, 2010), http://online.wsj.com/article/SB10001424052748703597204575483882585485368.html; *see also* Mark Mix, *Big Labor's Stealth Card-Check Strategy*, NATIONAL REVIEW (September 6, 2010), http://www.nationalreview.com/articles/245671/big-labor-s-stealth-card-check-strategy-mark-mix).

The *Dana Corp.* ruling involved the superiority of the secret ballot process compared to Card Check. Absent a federal law requiring card check, unions have persuaded certain employers to voluntarily allow Card Check. When employees unionize pursuant to a secret ballot, they cannot vote to decertify the union until the expiration of the first negotiated contract. In its *Dana* decision, the NLRB found Card Check to be a process inferior to the secret ballot and ruled that, where unionization has taken place pursuant to card check; within 45 days, the employees can force an immediate secret vote on whether they really want to join a union.

By deciding to reconsider the *Dana* ruling, the NLRB has raised the possibility that, without congressional action, Card Check will be put on an equal footing with the secret ballot process. It has also raised the possibility that the NLRB may attempt to impose Card Check on all employers leading to wide spread unionization with the potential for coercion and intimidation to obtain that result. Again, this raises uncertainty in the business community and discourages economic growth and job creation. As stated in Forbes: "[C]onsider what companies will do when forced to absorb labor costs higher than the market rate and higher than they can

JOB CREATION

afford. They certainly will not go hire more workers." (Brett Joshpe, *Fighting Card Check—And Winning*, FORBES (Jan. 8, 2009), http://www.forbes.com/2009/01/07/efca-labor-economy-oped-cx_bj_0108joshpe.html).

The Obama administrations relentless pursuit of business negative measures such as ObamaCare, Cap and Trade and Card Check have unquestionably created a sense of unease within the business community stifling both economic growth and job creation. While any of these measures standing alone would discourage entrepreneurial activity, taken as a group they demonstrate a pervasive anti-business attitude. Add to these initiatives the failure to extend the Bush tax cuts, the ever present threat of further tax increases, and pursuit of a regulatory agenda that increases government regulatory supervision of financial institutions but leaves the true culprits in the sub-prime mortgage debacle (Fannie Mae and Freddie Mac) unregulated, and you have a business environment so uncertain that American companies are reluctant to invest on new ventures or grow their existing businesses or payrolls. The result is a jobless recovery. To reverse this trend, the government must back off its economically destructive anti-business agenda and take positive action to foster a business friendly environment. The November 2010 election of a Republican controlled (and more economically conservative) House of Representatives, along with an increased number of economically conservative Senators should improve the business community's perception of the potential for further radical change. However, this may well be insufficient to generate meaningful certainty and job creation. As such, our four proposals for positive action are set forth below.

Four Proposals for Job Creation

We offer four proposals to strengthen *The Certainty Factor* for firms and individuals and support positive expectations for sales growth, better profitability, and improved household incomes.

JOB CREATION

Greater certainty about the future economic environment will incentivize businesses to increase investments, R+D, borrowing, and to make new purchases for plant, equipment, and other infrastructure. This will lead to significant job creation by the private sector, with private sector funds. Politicians and big government proponents need to step back from their current ideological and social agendas, their "father-knows-best" mentality, and remember what has always worked in the past. As such, we propose the following actions to significantly strengthen *The Certainty Factor*.

1 - Reduce Taxes & Overhaul/Simplify Tax Compliance
2 - Eliminate Regulations That Impede Economic Growth
3 - Dramatically Cut & Limit Government Spending
4 - Aggressively Expand Domestic Oil Production

These four initiatives are complementary, and will work together to instill greater confidence in the future prospects of the private sector, while building renewed investor optimism for corporate earnings and consumer spending. This will translate into an improved longer-term perspective for businesses to pursue expansion and new market opportunities, R+D spending, fixed asset investments, and better availability of commercial bank credit. Reductions in economic uncertainty will provide a strong catalyst for firms to create millions of new jobs throughout the private sector. As companies have improved profits and cash flow, they will have the capital necessary to pursue creativity and innovation in new products and services. This renewed optimism of *The Certainty Factor* is the basis for sustainable job creation, to meet the growth in both demand and supply.

Reduce, Overhaul, Simplify Taxes - *Increase Certainty*

British economist Adam Smith was completely correct in his famous *An Inquiry Into the Nature and Causes of The Wealth of Nations* (1776): "Complex tax codes are more burdensome to the

JOB CREATION

people than they are beneficial to the sovereign." Plainly and simply, individuals and businesses have to pay too many different taxes. Certain tax rates need to be significantly reduced, while other taxes and fees should simply be phased-out or eliminated altogether. Higher taxes and fees, and more of them, intercept a company's pre-tax operating income prior to showing a profit. For individuals, government taxes and fees intercept salaries and wages and significantly reduce take-home pay on average to just 75%-to-80% of gross earnings. The *Howard Jarvis Taxpayers Association* reminds businesses and individuals that they typically have to operate or work from January 1st until April or May or even June just to pay all the required taxes and fees government imposes on them. By siphoning off taxes and fees from the private sector, government cuts into what would otherwise be available for modernizing plant and equipment, R+D, saving, investing, business expansion, and creating jobs. Excessive taxes and fees also draw away funds from the capital market that could be available for loans and equity investments in firms and households. High current tax rates, and the prospects of both increasing those rates while adding new categories of taxes and fees, present greater risk to business planning and put significant negative pressure on *The Certainty Factor*. This erodes optimistic expectations about prospects for growth in sales and profits, and severely cripples (or eliminates) plans for hiring new workers.

On the following page, we summarize the eight taxes that the government must either reduce or eliminate. In addition, politicians have contemplated two other taxes the last few years as yet additional options to divert funds from the private sector and into government control. These should never be allowed on the floor of the House or Senate, as there can be no justifiable rationale for enacting additional burdens on the free flow of goods, services, and information within the U.S. economy. Cutting taxes across-the-board and eliminating/phasing out some in these eight categories would immediately signal great new opportunities for business profits and personal income, reduce business risk, and

JOB CREATION

TAXES REDUCED

Sales Tax-   Here in California it's 8.75%

Excise Tax-   Usage taxes on gasoline, gambling, tobacco

Property Tax-   Homeowners, business, commercial property owners pay annual percentage on value

Payroll Tax-   15.3% of each employee's wages/salary

Income Tax-   IRS, state and even city taxes 10% to 55%

Corporate Tax-   IRS, state, and even city taxes 15% to 39% - second highest in the world behind Japan

TAXES ELIMINATED

Capital Gains-   Tax value gains on a capital assets at 15%

Inheritance-   a.k.a. Estate or Death taxes at 37% to 55%

TAXES NEVER TO ENACT

National VAT-   The Value-Added Tax is a national sales tax in addition to state sales taxes. Popular in Europe. Built into prices of goods & services, raises all prices and eliminates existing jobs.

Internet Use-   Another excise tax on access to the web. Advocates want to levy a percentage fee on every online search, or purchase, or login. Others want a flat annual usage fee.

JOB CREATION

strengthen expectations for both companies and individuals in the private sector. The improved *Certainty Factor* would provide excellent incentives to pursue innovation, modernize plant and equipment, increase R+D, and hire more and more workers, for both the near-term and longer-term. Taken together, government has invaded virtually every aspect of individual and business activities by assessing a tax or fee that becomes revenue for a local, state, or federal government to spend.

Consider the mind-numbing ramifications of this one individual example for John and Mary Citizen here in California. They purchase $30,000 of goods and services each year (not including gas for their two cars) that are taxed at 8.75% by their state ($2,625). They have combined gross income of $100,000 and taxable income of $60,000 and pay $19,700 to the IRS and $5,700 to Sacramento, and they have $7,650 in payroll taxes taken out of their checks. Their house is worth $375,000 and they pay $4,400 in property taxes. Their gasoline is taxed at 63.9 cents per gallon (over 20% of the $3.09/gallon cost for 87 unleaded), so they paid another $610 on the 950 gallons they bought during the year. So they pay total taxes of $40,685 from their $100,000 annual combined income, or just under 41% of everything they make. But what if California reduced its sales tax over the short-term to just 3% - that would result in $1,725 of additional funds staying in their household, rather than being paid in sales taxes to the state. If their federal income tax rate was dropped to 15% and their state income tax rate to 5%, they would save another $10,700 and $2,700 respectively, or $13,400 of additional funds staying in the household. If their property tax rates were reduced to a flat across-the-board one percent (1%), they would save another $650 in taxes. If California reduced the gas tax to 30 cents per gallon, they would save another $280 in gas taxes. And if the payroll tax was reduced to a combined 10% (half paid by the employer and half by the employee), they would save another $2,650 in taxes withheld from their paychecks. Their total annual tax savings would then be $18,705 - about one-fifth their annual gross income, they could then use for savings, investing, consumer purchases, home improvements, tuition and other related costs for their own continuing education, tuition for one or more of their kids who are in private school or college, a nice vacation, and perhaps a new car every three years.

Over the years, the savings they put away, and the investments they could make in stocks, bonds, mutual funds, and/or property would not be subject to capital gains taxation when they hold their assets for more than one year. When their kids inherit investments and assets after their death, they will not only see a larger after-tax estate (less taxes paid over time), but with estate taxes eliminated, that intra-family wealth transfer would facilitate their heirs making new rounds of investments, savings, home improvements, and large scale consumer purchases.

The same general evaluation holds true for large corporations. "America's corporate tax rate is very high by global standards, and reducing it would improve U.S. competitiveness and boost economic performance. America is also one of the few nations that double-taxes corporate income earned in other nations, thus exacerbating the damage caused by high marginal tax rates." (Daniel Mitchell, *Competitiveness Means Less Government, Not More*, HERITAGE FOUNDATION (April 20, 2006), http://www.heritage.org/research/reports/2006/04/competitiveness-means-less-government-not-more). The U.S. also "double-taxes" corporations, first with income tax and then taxes on the dividends paid to shareholders. Consider a firm doing $800 million in sales, with $300 million in pre-tax income. Currently, it pays a combined 45% in federal and state income taxes ($135 million), plus $15.3 million in payroll withholding taxes on its employees (not to mention various sales and excise taxes on its business transactions, plus property tax on its offices and plant). It then pays a dividend to its shareholders from the after-tax profit, which the government again taxes as income to the shareholder.

JOB CREATION

If the corporate taxes rates were reduced to a combined 25%, along with the reduced payroll withholding, the firm would realize over $66 million in higher after-tax earnings. Those funds could be allocated to new plant and equipment, which would result in more people being hired not only at that company, but also at firms that make the equipment and build the new facility. Other funds could be spent on R+D to design and create new products and services. Investors in the firm could receive larger dividends paid on their shares (remember, the U.S. "double taxes" corporate income and dividends). With lower taxes or no taxes on gains in stock prices plus dividend income, individual shareholders and institutional investors such as mutual funds, pension funds, and insurance portfolios would have more capital to invest and/or spend in the economy. Firms would have additional cash flow with which to engage in multiple levels of commercial transactions with each other, and improved internally generated capital (retained earnings) with which to expand and hire more workers.

For both individual taxpayers and corporations, the basic principle is the same. Lower tax rates across-the-board put more money in the hands of the private sector to save, spend, and invest in the economy. Of course that initially looks like less tax revenues for city, county, state, and federal governments. However, in the next chapter, we examine the net effect of lower tax *rates* on a growing economy to potentially produce more total tax *revenue*. A snapshot of this took place just recently when in 2003, President Bush cut both the dividend and capital gains tax rates to 15 percent, and strong economic growth followed. These two cuts generated a huge windfall between 2004 and 2007, as federal tax revenues increased by $785 billion, the largest four-year increase in American history. Tax revenues climbed twice as fast as the Bush Administration had predicted (up more than $250 billion), so that the budget deficit actually declined by over $100 billion. (Edmund L. Andrews, *Surprising Jump in Tax Revenues Is Curbing Deficit*, N.Y. TIMES

JOB CREATION

(July 9, 2006), http://www.nytimes.com/ 2006/07/09/washington/ 09econ.html). The U.S. Treasury reported that individual and corporate income tax receipts were up 40 percent in the three years following the Bush tax cuts, and the "rich" (top marginal tax-rate individual taxpayers) paid an even higher percentage of the total tax burden than they had at any time in at least the previous 40 years. By 2005, the stock market was up 20%, and by 2006, $15 trillion of new private sector investment wealth had been created, and the U.S. economy added 8 million new jobs by 2007, while the median U.S. household increased wealth by $20,000 in *real* terms. (Ryan Dwyer, *Bush Tax Cuts Boosted Federal Revenue*, WASHINGTON TIMES (February 3, 2010), http://www.washingtontimes.com/news/2010/feb/3/bush-tax-cuts-boosted-federal-revenue/). Fourteen states do not have an income tax - Washington, Alaska, Florida, Nevada, New Hampshire, South Dakota, Tennessee, Texas, and Wyoming. Combined they had an average 18.2% growth rate in jobs over the past decade, more than twice the 8.4% job growth of the nine states with the highest income tax rates. The Seattle Times accurately describes the state's zero income tax as "a selling point, an asset, and more than that, it's a bonus for living here", as Democratic Governor Christine Gregoire begins her public presentation sales pitch to all prospective business investors thinking about Washington state, with the reminder: "No income tax" (Scott Stanzel, *"No Income Tax!" Touts Gov. Gregoire's Department of Commerce*, RED COUNTY (Aug. 8, 2010), http://www.redcounty.com/content/% E2%80%9Cno-income-tax%E2%80%9D-touts-gov-gregoire%E2%80%99s-department-commerce).

The typical response to *any* proposal like ours to dramatically cut taxes is that such reductions are impossible to fathom. Politicians always panic because they understand it means a reduction in the funds available for them to spend on the endless lists of social programs, entitlements, and other special interests. They are unable to comprehend that lowering tax rates could

JOB CREATION

actually generate more tax revenue on a larger, growing economy. Remember, it's not as if lost tax funds somehow disappear from the U.S. economy. The larger corporate profits and household take-home pay will show up in a wide range of economic activities like savings, investments, consumer spending, business purchases – rather than government allocations, and result in more jobs. Granted, a portion of government spending occurs in the private sector; for example, defense appropriations are paid to Boeing, Raytheon, United Technologies, and TRW. But a large portion of tax dollars pay for price subsidies, welfare, jobless benefits and other entitlements, education, labor, funds transfers, and around 22% to debt service (interest the U.S. Treasury must pay on outstanding T-Bills, T-Notes, and 30-year T-Bonds). But the key component to see lower tax rates turn into more tax revenues is significant reductions in government spending.

Today, many economists and policy analysts suggest something similar to the successful tax cuts by Ronald Reagan in the 1980s, and similarly successful Kennedy tax cuts in the 1960s. Both of these were very successful and therefore should be implemented over tax rebates or credits. (Peter Ferrara, *Tax Cuts Would Really Stimulate*, FORBES (February 4, 2004), http://www.forbes.com/2009/02/04/tax-cut-stimulus-opinions-contributors_0204_peter_ferrara.html). Many economists believe a cut in the corporate tax rate should be implemented rather than another stimulus. "The U.S. rate is second only to Japan's -- another country that's failed to create enough new jobs in recent years; reducing the corporate tax rate from 35 percent to 25 percent, while keeping the capital gains tax at 15 percent, could create an average of at least 2 million jobs a year over the next decade." (Edwin Feulner, *Making the Number Who Hire Go Higher*, TOWNHALL.COM (April 19, 2010), http://townhall.com/columnists/EdFeulner/2010/04/20/making_the_number_who_hire_go_higher). The evidence for the positive impact that tax cuts have on the economy and job creation is overwhelming. In

JOB CREATION

March 1975 President Gerald Ford signed tax cuts into law and marked the bottom of a recession that month. He heeded advice from Arthur Laffer that tax cuts increase incentives to work and spur economic growth. The Dow jumped back up to the near 1000, a big leap from the near 100 when he began office. Jimmy Carter ignored Ford's example and left office with a lower Dow than when he arrived. Reagan initiated tax cuts and the Dow shot up beyond 1000. So what is the lesson to be learned? Tax cuts always equate to economic growth. (D. Luskin, *Ford's Legacy Is the Idea that Tax Cuts Stimulate the Economy*, SMART MONEY (January 2, 2007), www.smartmoney.com/investing/ stocks/fords-legacy-is-the-idea-that-tax-cuts-stimulate-the-economy-20574/).

The current U.S. individual and corporate tax code is extremely complicated, filled with thousands of loopholes, overly burdensome on taxpayer compliance, and in many cases taxes the same income twice. Following is a sample of the top individual tax rates over the last one hundred years shows the random folly of politicians in imposing their penalties against being successful in private sector endeavors.

100 YEARS OF TOP PERSONAL INCOME TAX RATES

1913:	7%
1920:	73%
1930:	25%
1940:	81%
1950:	84%
1960:	91%
1970:	72%
1980:	70%
1990:	28%
2000:	39%
2010:	35%

JOB CREATION

What kind of political mindset conceives of and implements tax rates that take away from private sector individuals and businesses 73%, 81%, or 91% of their earnings? Where is the logic in destroying the profit incentive by "allowing" enterprising individuals and firms to keep only 27%, 19%, or just 9% of what they make from their hard work? The burden is further exacerbated by the 7,500 pages, and over 3.4 million words, that explain the U.S. tax code to taxpayers. The directions for filing a 1040 tax form covers 161 pages. The IRS employs just over 100,000 workers and has an annual budget in excess of $11 billion. More than $3.5 billion is spent by U.S. firms on tax-related lobbying of Congress in Washington. Over half of individual taxpayers hire someone to do their filings because the tax laws are essentially incomprehensible, resulting in accountants and other tax preparers preparing and filing 80 million tax returns. Most or all of those funds could be re-allocated to productive enterprise activities such as R+D to create and develop new goods and services, market expansion, and a wide range of technology improvements throughout the economy. Existing federal and state tax rates and codes unequivocally penalize the success of both individuals and businesses. Simplifying the tax code and reducing both the number of taxes and the amount of tax we pay would go a long way towards increasing positive economic certainty in the business community generating growth and jobs.

Eliminate Regulations – *Increase Certainty*

It is time to conduct a meaningful cost-benefit analysis designed to eliminate those regulations that impede economic growth with minimal benefit(s). Government regulation is pervasive in both the American business community and American life in general. The Office of Advocacy of the U.S. Small Business Administration reported, "[a] comprehensive list of regulatory influences that affect one's daily existence is indeed extensive and overwhelming to track or sum up" (U.S. SMALL BUS. ADMIN. OFFICE OF ADVOCACY,

JOB CREATION

SBAHQ-08-M-0466, THE IMPACT OF REGULATORY COSTS ON SMALL FIRMS (2010), *available at* https://docs.google.com/viewer?url=http://www.sba.gov/advo/research/rs371tot.pdf (SBA Report)). The SBA Report goes on to note that such costs are "relatively hidden" and that "[t]he costs of government regulation gets stirred into the indistinct mixture of countless economic forces that determine prices, costs, designs, locations, profits, losses, wages, dividends, and so forth" (See: SBA Report).

While some regulation is certainly necessary to assure that the free market remains free and that government can fulfill its obligation to "provide for the . . . general Welfare" (U.S. CONST. art. I, § 8), overregulation is smothering American economic growth. The only rational solution is to both reduce the number and end the proliferation of regulations that fail to produce benefits sufficient to justify their costs. To do so meaningfully, we need to limit current regulatory initiatives to those necessary for national defense and protecting the public safety as we conduct an independent bipartisan analysis of the costs and benefits (financial and societal) of our current regulatory structure with the stated goal of reducing overregulation and thereby reducing the cost of starting and operating a business in America. We also need to take a serious look at the mindset that led us from being a nation of independent entrepreneurs building the greatest economy in history to a nation burdened by a regulatory bureaucracy so pervasive that it is strangling our entrepreneurial spirit. The business of America should be business, not bureaucracy.

The regulatory burdens on any existing business and any entrepreneur considering opening a new business are extensive and oppressive. As long ago as 27 years, in 1993, the Cato Institute issued a Policy Analysis covering the opening of a simple dry cleaning business. Even then the regulatory environment was making it "increasingly difficult to maintain a small business" and "even more difficult to start one." (Jonathan H. Adler, *Taken to the Cleaners: A Case Study of the Overregulation of American Small*

JOB CREATION

Business, CATO INSTITUTE (December 22, 1993), http://www.cato.org/pub_display.php?pub_id=1059). This analysis noted that opening a new dry-cleaning shop could "require filling out and complying with 100 forms and manuals" and that "[e]nvironmental and other regulation [could] increase start-up costs as much as $138,700 and impose burdensome permitting and reporting requirements." (*Taken to the Cleaners*, CATO INSTITUTE, Dec. 22, 1993). It concluded that "[t]he experience of the dry-cleaning industry with government regulation is indicative of the general concerns faced by today's small business owners and entrepreneurs. Because of the important role of small businesses and entrepreneurship in the creation of jobs and economic opportunity, the present trend should be of great concern to policymakers." (*Taken to the Cleaners*, CATO INSTITUTE, Dec. 22, 1993). Unfortunately, policymakers failed to heed the Cato Institute's warning as the regulatory environment has subsequently become both more burdensome and more costly.

To open and operate a typical quick service restaurant, an entrepreneur-franchisee must comply with a vast array of local, state and federal regulations. The next page shows the basic checklist covering the 57 general categories of federal, state and local regulations with which an entrepreneur must comply to open and operate a restaurant divided by: 1) site selection, 2) pre-operation, and 3) operation requirements (yes, that's *57!!* separate legislated requirements and compliance regulations). This is not a list of specific regulations but rather general categories of regulations. The list of regulations itself would be far lengthier. It is difficult to cover all the categories of various state and local regulations because they vary by jurisdiction. (See: *The 'Boxes' Schwarzenegger Didn't Get Around To Blowing Up,* Investors.com (November 12, 2010) http://www.investors.com/newsandanalysis/article.aspx?id=553704). However, this sequence captures the general areas regulated and typical timeframe that are required by some form of governmental agency. Many of these regulations are necessary and provide societal or financial benefits

175

JOB CREATION

57 Regulatory Categories to Open & Operate ONE Restaurant

A. SITE SELECTION REQUIREMENTS
(4 months to 2 years, average around 6 months)
1. General Comment Regarding Governing Law, including FDA 1999 Food Code 2. Preliminary Due Diligence 3. Site Zoning then 4. Parking ratio then 5. Setbacks + easements, then 6. Signage, 7. Drive-thru Approval, and 8. Hours of operation 9. Site Access and 10. Utilities Availability-Capacity 11. Site Conditions, including: 12. Soils tests 13. Wetlands review 14. Land disturbance permit 15. Water table 16. State EPA 17. Water management review 18. Storm water 19. Coastal Commission 20. Environ Impact 21. Archeological/Native American artifacts

B. PRE-OPERATING REQUIREMENTS
(5 to 12 months, average around 9 months)
22. Site Development and 23. Site plan approval 24. All applicable inspections and permits, 25. Occupancy permit, 26. food manager's certificate, 27. fire department, 28. Comply with applicable energy laws (e.g., Title 24 energy codes in California), 29. State organizational documents (corporation, LLC, partnership), 30. Fictitious name registrations, 31. Certificate of authority to do business, 32. Federal Employer ID Number from IRS, 33. State business and 34. Employment taxes,35. State and 36. Local real and personal property taxes, 37. State workers compensation insurance registration, 38. State-temporary disability insurance/registration, 39. State franchise laws.

C. OPERATION REQUIREMENTS (ongoing)
40. Food Safety Laws, 41. Federal, 42. State, 43. Local health food codes, 44. Labeling, and 45. Advertising laws. 46. Comply with carriers, 47. Environmental, 48. Air Quality, and 49. Waste laws, 50. OSHA, 51. Employment, 52. Hiring, 53. Pension & Welfare, 54. Disability, 55. Military, 56. Workers' Compensation, and 57. Antitrust requirements.

commensurate with their costs. Nonetheless, many are unnecessarily burdensome or superfluous and the result of a nanny state mentality that places a government bureaucracy in the position of managing the minutest of details in the creation and operation of what primarily should be entrepreneurial ventures. Let's face reality; the government is incapable of starting or operating a profitable self-sustaining business. Yet, as demonstrated above, through legislation and regulation the government's role in almost every aspect of an American private sector business even as simple as a quick service restaurant has become pervasive and prohibitive.

Rather than detailing certain onerous and useless regulations, our focus here will be on the costs of government performing this vast regulatory function and the need to limit current regulatory initiatives to those necessary for national defense and public safety as we conduct a critical analysis of the costs and benefits of our current regulatory framework as well as the political philosophy that got us to where we are.

The cost of complying with the pervasive rules and regulations American businesses face today is overwhelming and increasing at a disturbing rate. According to the SBA Report, "[t]he cost of federal regulation in the United States increased to more than $1.75 trillion in 2008." (SBA Report at iv). Perhaps as disturbing, 2008's $1.75 trillion cost for federal regulation represents an inflation adjusted increase in regulatory costs of $43 billion just since 2004. (SBA Report at 7). Notably, the SBA Report deals solely with federal regulations and fails to include the extensive costs of state and local rules, regulations and requirements. The SBA Report itself notes that it does not capture such costs and that "[r]egulatory agencies in the 50 American states have promulgated hundreds of thousands of regulations that are superimposed on federal regulations." (SBA Report at 13). Based on a series of recent studies in eight U.S. cities, the Institute for Justice concluded that "one of the principal obstacles to creating new jobs and entrepreneurial activity in cities across the country is the complex maze of regulations cities and states impose on small businesses." (*City Studies: Government Barriers to Entrepreneurship*, INSTITUTE FOR JUSTICE, http://www.ij.org/citystudies; *see also Licensing to Kill*, WALL STREET JOURNAL (October 25, 2010), http://online.wsj.com/article/SB10001424052702304741404575564171912051184.html). In addition, the SBA Report covers 2008 and fails to include even federal (let alone state and local) legislation and regulation implemented since that time. Thus, for example, it fails to include regulatory costs associated with the recently enacted financial reform legislation or any of the extensive costs that are or will be associated with ObamaCare. Finally, the SBA Report fails to include the indirect or secondary costs of regulation. For example, environmental regulations directly affect the cost of producing electricity and the SBA Report includes such costs as direct costs for utilities. However, such "increases in the costs of electricity have ripple effects throughout the American economy in the form of higher energy costs thus indirectly raising costs in virtually every sector" and the SBA Report does not include these ripple effect costs (SBA Report at 15). As such, the $1.75 trillion total cost of regulation in the SBA Report, while overwhelming, is clearly understated.

As the SBA Report notes, 2008's $1.75 trillion cost of federal regulation, understated though it is, represented "14 percent of US national income" (SBA Report at 6). When "combined with US federal tax receipts, which equated to 21% of national income in 2008, these two costs consumed 35 percent of national income" (SBA Report at 6). That means we were paying one out of every three dollars earned in American in 2008 to pay for or comply with federal government programs. If these costs were equally divided among each American household it would have amounted to $37,962 per household. (Nicole V. Crain & W. Mark Crain, *The Regulation Tax Keeps Growing*, WALL ST. J. (Sept. 27, 2010), http://online.wsj.com/article/SB10001424052748703860104575

JOB CREATION

5508122499819564.html). The additional burden of state and local regulations plus federal legislation and regulations enacted since 2008 can only dramatically increase this cost in real dollars and as a percentage of national income.

To put even this $1.75 trillion in perspective, if just this cost were divided equally among every American household, each household would have owed $15,586 in 2008. "By comparison, the federal regulatory burden exceeds by 50 percent private spending on health care which equaled $10,500 per household in 2008" (SBA Report at iv). "The portion of regulatory costs that falls initially on businesses was $8,086 per employee in 2008" (SBA Report at iv). However, such costs are distributed unequally among large and small American businesses. The SBA Report defines "small businesses" as businesses employing less than 20 workers. Small businesses make up 89% of all firms in the U.S. (SBA Report at 6) and such small businesses "face an annual regulatory cost of $10,585 per employee" as compared to larger businesses, nearly 25% higher than the national average (SBA Report at iv). As many of the costs associated with regulatory compliance are fixed costs, larger firms are able to spread these costs over a larger employee base and reduce their per employee costs (SBA Report at 8). As such, "on almost every regulatory frontier, compliance costs place small businesses at a competitive disadvantage (SBA Report at 57). Because the brunt of the costs associated with regulatory compliance fall on smaller businesses, which include most start up businesses, these costs fall where they can least be borne and have a substantial negative impact on entrepreneurial creation of new companies and new jobs.

The enormity of this $1.75 trillion burden on our economy represents government's view of the appropriate division of responsibility between the private sector and government itself. The question is whether $1.75 trillion (an amount in excess of even our recent enormous annual $1.42 trillion and $1.29 trillion budget deficits) or 14% percent of our entire nation income is worth what we get in exchange for this regulatory function. From those in government whose power and employment depend on the continued existence and expansion of the government's regulatory function, the answer would understandably be "yes." From those in the business community whose profits and growth are impaired by this regulatory function, the answer is just as understandably "no." The real answer lies somewhere in between and requires a cost-benefits analysis of existing legislation and regulation which, to date, no one has meaningfully accomplished.

Nonetheless, there are a number of things we do know. First, it should be obvious to anyone that expending $1.75 trillion or 14% of our national income on regulatory compliance is simply too much, exceeding even our enormous annual budget deficits and the per household amount we spend each year on healthcare (which the Obama Administration considered a national emergency). This is particularly true in light of the fact that this amount is grossly understated as it fails to include the costs of state and local business regulation, regulations or legislation enacted since 2008 and the ancillary costs of regulation. In other words, the impact on the economy is certainly greater than even 14% of national income or $1.75 trillion. To say that these costs fall on firms and are a reasonable cost of doing business ignores the reality that these costs are now so high that they discourage and even prohibit business growth and that "all regulatory costs are – and can only be – borne by individuals, as consumers, as workers, as stockholders, as owners or as taxpayers" (SBA Report at 36). In other words, we all pay these costs.

Any rational person must recognize that some regulation is necessary for government to fulfill its intended function and, at the same time, that American business is simply over regulated. The real question is whether, on a law by law, regulation by regulation basis, we get a societal benefit commensurate with the regulatory cost. To answer this question meaningfully, we need a comprehensive, independent, non-partisan cost-benefit analysis performed by individuals with no vested interest in the outcome or by a panel balanced between those in government and those in business. We also need a Congress and a President willing to make the tough choices required to reduce these out of control costs that inhibit business, economic growth and job creation.

Congress acknowledged the need for and the potential benefits of conducting such a cost-benefits analysis when it enacted the Regulatory-Right-To-Know Act. 31 U.S.C. sec. 1105. Pursuant to this law, the Office of Management and Budget ("OMB") has been preparing an annual report to Congress since 1997 on the Benefits and Costs of Federal Regulations. However, these Reports are of limited benefit. As the OMB notes in its 2009 Report, "because these estimates exclude non major rules and rules adopted more than 10 years ago, the total benefits and costs of all Federal rules now in effect are likely to be significantly larger than the sum of the benefits and costs reported. . . ." (U.S. OFFICE OF MANAGEMENT AND BUDGET, OFFICE OF INFORMATION AND REGULATORY AFFAIRS, 2009 REPORT TO CONGRESS ON THE COSTS AND BENEFITS OF FEDERAL REGULATIONS AND UNFUNDED MANDATES ON STATE, LOCAL AND TRIBAL ENTITIES, *available at* https://docs.google.com/viewer?url= http://www.whitehouse.gov/sites/default/files/omb/assets/legislative_ reports/2009_final_BC_Report_01272010.pdf (OMBReport)). Ignoring rules adopted over 10 years ago excludes some of the most costly federal regulations including certain of the regulations under the Clean Air Act and its amendments. In addition, the estimates the OMB relies upon are themselves questionable as the sources for such estimates are the same federal agencies tasked with promulgating and enforcing those regulations. The OMB Report also excludes non-major regulations which, taken in the aggregate, could be substantial, and regulations issued by independent agencies (agencies outside the executive branch). It also excludes state and local regulations. As the Report itself states, "[w]hile the estimates in this Report provide valuable information about the effects of regulations, they should not be taken to be either precise or complete. OMB continues to consider methods for increasing the accuracy of benefit-cost analysis" (OMB Report at 4; *see also* SBA Report at 2-5). In other words, while this cost/benefits analysis is of limited use, it is somewhat of a start.

The impact of overregulation on American business is overwhelming. To create certainty in the business community that our government is supportive of private sector growth and private sector job creation, we must reduce the pervasive bureaucracy that currently deems its mission to control or extinguish the American entrepreneurial spirit and we must eliminate regulations whose costs bear little or no relationship to their financial or societal benefits and which impose government created barriers to free enterprise. Finally, we must adopt a vision of government and free enterprise that places government's role in a more realistic and limited perspective. The first step in this process is a meaningful independent cost-benefits analysis that can serve as a basis for regulatory reduction. Thomas Jefferson wisely predicted future happiness for Americans "if we can prevent the government from wasting the labors of the people under the pretense of taking care of them. . . ." (Letter from Thomas Jefferson to Thomas Cooper (Nov. 29, 1802), *in* 2 Thomas Jefferson: Writings, 1110 (Eaton Press, 1993)). These are words our Congress and our President would be well advised to heed.

Cut and Limit Government Spending - *Increase Certainty*

Our third proposal requires the federal government to dramatically reduce its spending across the board, and in many cases eliminate spending in many of the programs that consistently consumed tax resources without any tangible, measureable benefits. It is time to rein in runaway government entitlements, appropriations, subsidies, grants, regulations and those pet projects of Senators and Representatives that are often loaded with additional spending amendments to benefit their home state constituents (and bolster their re-election prospects),

JOB CREATION

or to satisfy special interests and lobbyists. This kind of proposal has often been called for, but has very rarely, if ever, been implemented. We must radically change the entrenched mentality of unnecessary spending programs that get into one budget, and end up staying there for years.

The history of income taxes in America is fascinating to review, as the initiation was always viewed as a temporary way to raise money. First, the income tax was a flat three percent (3%) to pay down government debt associated with the Civil War, which Congress repealed once it paid. In 1894, Congress put a two percent (2%) peacetime income tax went into effect but only about one in ten Americans made enough to pay it. The logic behind the income tax progressed into a constitutional amendment giving Congress the "power to lay and collect taxes on incomes" that, since the end of WWII, has driven continued escalation of government spending without regard for the economic impacts. (U.S. Const. amend. XIV).

Government has now assumed an ever-increasing role in both transferring and confiscating income and wealth from private sector individual and corporate taxpayers to fund legislated spending and related regulatory administration based upon a perspective that the government's goals and objectives supersede the role of private enterprise, the *invisible hand,* and capital market funding in developing new job opportunities. Matthew Continetti captured this mindset, that "in the liberal imagination, our earnings are the government's by default, and the president and Congress determine through the tax code how much to give back to the people" (Matthew Continetti, *Obama's Tax Evasion*, THE WEEKLY STANDARD (September 27, 2010), http://www.weekly standard.com/articles/obama%E2%80%99s-tax-evasion). Deficit spending has become the norm for government fiscal policy. Rather than utilize Treasury debt for a one-time or limited-term emergency appropriation (e.g., paying for a war, or recovering

JOB CREATION

from a natural disaster), politicians regularly spend even more than the government collects in taxes, and the annual budget deficit is simply added year-by-year to the total outstanding balance of unpaid federal debt.

During the first eight years of the 21st century, the Bush Administration incurred an average $260 billion in annual deficits, adding $2.08 trillion to the national debt. This period included the recovery years right after the terrorist attacks of 9/11, the invasion and overthrow of the Taliban in Afghanistan, and the subsequent Operation Iraqi Freedom. By contrast, the Obama Administration has incurred a $1.4 trillion deficit just for fiscal 2009, and then a projected $1.29 trillion deficit for 2010, adding $2.7 trillion to the national debt in just two years. "Projections for financing just one half of Obama's health care initiative over the next decade will fall roughly $50 billion below expectations, so to fill this revenue gap, [Obama has proposed] several new ideas for raising [another] $60 billion over 10 years, mainly from tightening rules for inheritance taxes, but also from changes in taxing some types of life insurance and other products" (Jackie Calmes, *U.S. Budget Deficit Is Revised to Surpass $1.8 Trillion*, N.Y. TIMES (May 11, 2009), http://www.nytimes.com/ 2009/05/12/business/ economy/12budget.html).

The unparalleled levels of government spending have huge negative ramifications for the future financial stability of the U.S., private sector capital markets, and job creation. The numbers are very clear. Any citizen can review just how bad it is by looking at the back page of the IRS taxpayer's 1040 booklet. For 2009, one quarter (23%) is spent on the military, forty percent is spent on combined social security (20%) and Medicare/Medicaid (19%). Other required entitlement spending is 17%, leaving only 12% for non-mandatory discretionary spending. (See: *2009 IRS Individual Tax Preparation Guide*, Source: Office of Management and Budget). Interest on the total debt was $383 billion in 2009 and $414

JOB CREATION

billion in 2010. (*Interest Rate on the Debt Outstanding*, U.S. Dept. of the Treasury, Bureau of the Public Debt (November 3, 2010) http://www.treasurydirect.gov/govt/reports/ir/ir_expense.htm).

Based on our analysis and in line with other forecasts and reviews, we project government's out of control deficit spending to create between a $1.1 and $1.3 trillion deficit in 2011, with the potential to be $1.3 to $1.5 trillion of red ink in 2012. While the baseline numbers on most estimates for 2011 and 2012 remain in the range of $1 trillion, the significant additional entitlement requirements to fully fund ObamaCare combined with increasingly likely expectations for slow/anemic growth due to so much uncertainty, are harbingers that deficits could very well remain over $1 trillion through the end of this decade. Numerous models and reports project just under $10 trillion of total new debt being added in the upcoming decade, which would push the national debt to more than $23 trillion by 2020. (See, *The Budget and Economic Outlook: Fiscal Years 2010 to 2020*, Congressional Budget Office, Office of Management and Budget Report (January 2010) http://www.cbo.gov/ftpdocs/108xx/doc10871/Frontmatter.sht ml; Mid-Session Review, Budget of The U.S. Government Fiscal Year 2011, Office of Management and Budget (July 23, 2010) http://www.whitehouse.gov/sites/default/files/omb/assets/fy20 11_msr/ 11msr.pdf; *How does Obama's projected 2011 budget compare?* Los Angeles Times (February 1, 2010) http://articles.latimes.com/2010 /feb/01/nation/la-na-budget-deficit2-2010feb02; *CBO report: Debt will rise to 90% of GDP*, Washington Times (March 26, 2010) www.washingtontimes.com/news/2010/mar/26/cbos-2020-vision-debt-will-rise-to-90-of-gdp; *Inflation, Deficit Spending and the 2011 U.S. Budget*, Seeking Alpha (February 1, 2010) http://seekingalpha.com/article/185786-inflation-deficit-spending-and-the-2011-u-s-budget).

Tremendous uncertainty for individuals and businesses about the negative fiscal impact of Obama's health care spending fuels much

JOB CREATION

of this, but the basic budget math is easy to do. If today's historically low Treasury rates were still in place in 2020, interest on the debt would balloon to over $560 billion - 15% of the total projected 2020 budget. If continued inflationary pressures from so much debt were to increase Treasury rates over the next several years, each additional one percentage point increase requires another $200 billion in interest expenses from the federal budget. "If taxes are held at historic levels, entitlement spending will by 2052 consume the entire federal budget, leaving nothing for the national defense or even interest on our debt mountain." (Theodore Bromund, *I'm Afraid to Tell You There's No Money Left*, THE FOUNDRY (May 19, 2010), http://blog.heritage.org/2010/05/19/im-afraid-to-tell-you-theres-no-money-left/).

The increasing size of the federal work force is an early indication of what lies ahead. The Bureau of Labor Statistics reports that in the last year the federal government added 86,000 permanent (non-Census) jobs to the rolls and high-paying jobs at that. The number of federal salaries over $100,000 per year has increased by nearly 50% since the beginning of the recession. Today, the average federal worker earns 77% more than the average private-sector worker, according to a USA Today analysis of data from the federal Office of Personnel Management (Arthur Brooks, *Slouching Towards Athens*, WALL STREET JOURNAL (June 5, 2010), http://online.wsj.com/article/SB10001424052748704764404575286451653109876.html). From the start of the recession in 2008, the federal government has added 198,000 new jobs (+10%) to its taxpayer-funded payrolls, while the private sector has lost 7.83 million jobs (*Since the Recession, Private Sector Employment Tumbled While Federal Employment Grew*," Heritage Foundation (August 6, 2010) www.heritage.org/multimedia/infographic/2010/08/since-the-recession-private-sector-employment-tumbled-while-federal-employment-grew). To pay for bigger government, the private sector will continue to bear a heavier tax burden far into the future, suppressing the innovation and entrepreneurship that creates growth and real opportunity, not to mention the tax revenue that pays for everything else in the first place. If these trends continue, it is hard to see how our culture of free enterprise will survive, as we know it.

Until the government runs out of money or the ability to borrow, more and more young Americans will grow more accustomed to a system where the government pays better wages, offers the best job protection, allows the earliest retirement, and guarantees the most lavish pensions. Against such competition, young would-be entrepreneurs will inevitably choose the safety and comfort of government employment—and do so with all the drive that is generally thought to be "good enough" for that kind of work. (Arthur Brooks, *Slouching Toward Athens*, WALL STREET JOURNAL (June 5, 2010), http:// online.wsj.com/article/ SB10001424052748704764404575286451653109876.html).

Expand Domestic Oil – *Increase Certainty*

Our fourth proposal is focused directly on expanding every facet of domestic energy production, particularly oil production. The Obama administration's distain for fossil fuels has created great uncertainty in the private sector over the future cost of energy, the availability of energy in the amounts needed to sustain economic growth and the undependable nature of our reliance on foreign energy sources. While pursuing alternative so-called "clean energy" sources is certainly an admirable endeavor, such alternative sources are currently economically unfeasible and produce energy insufficient to meaningfully offset our need for fossil fuels, particularly oil. Nuclear power is certainly a meaningful, feasible, and proven energy source that we should vigorously pursue. However, even this energy source has encountered strong resistance from environmentalists. Natural gas is another very viable low carbon emissions alternative energy source. (*See*, G. Gilder, *California's Destructive Green Energy Lobby*,

JOB CREATION

The Wall Street Journal (November 16, 2010) http://online.wsj.com/article_email/SB1000142405274870330404575610402116987146MyQjAxMTAwMDEwODExNDgyWj.html). Yet, to restore energy confidence in the private sector and to encourage economic growth while simultaneously pursuing viable clean energy alternatives, we need to increase reliance on our domestic oil supply and reduce reliance on unstable and unreliable foreign sources. The uncertainty of reliance on foreign oil is a significant impediment to investment in our economy and confidence about our economic future.

First, the U.S. needs to build dozens of new oil refineries. Second, we must modernize and expand the national system of pipelines and storage facilities, from ports and fields through to holding and distribution. Finally, we must immediately initiate domestic oil exploration and development of new oil fields in order to ensure that America will have a strong and reliable energy foundation for the future, both to support continued domestic economic growth, and for improving energy self-reliance in an increasingly risky geopolitical world. This exploration and development must occur in America's clearly identified untapped offshore reserves, as well as the significant potential oil reservoirs within the Alaskan National Wildlife Refuge (ANWR). The U.S. produces about 4.95 million barrels per day of crude oil, but has to import 9.78 million barrels to meet daily demand of just over 14.5 million - its top four sources being: Canada (2.2 million/day), Saudi Arabia (1.35m), Mexico (1m), and Nigeria (1m). (*See:* U.S. Energy Information Administration ("EIA") report (August 23, 2010); www.EIA.DOE.gov; *For example*: http://www.eia.doe.gov/pub/oil_gas/petroleum/datapublications/company_level_imports/current/import.html). So we are currently producing one third and importing two thirds. We spend over $700 billion per year on that imported crude oil. We also hold 4.2 billion barrels of crude in our strategic reserve - about a 9-10 month supply. (See: www.EIA.DOE.gov). For relative perspective, Saudi Arabia has the largest proven crude oil reserves (297 billion barrels), and Canada is second (179

JOB CREATION

billion barrels). The Minerals Management Service (MMS) reported in 2008 the U.S. has about 18 billion barrels in contiguous offshore reserves (which have been banned by Congress from development since 1982), over 85 billion barrels in the outer continental shelf, including the Gulf of Mexico, and another 40 billion barrels off the coasts of Alaska and California. (See: www.EIA.DOE.gov). This totals 143 billion barrels in untapped crude reserves, or roughly 40 years worth relative to replacing half of the 9.78 million barrels per day of imported crude. Opening new drilling and development projects today in the oil industry would start to produce new domestic crude by 2015. The targeted 5 million new barrels per day would replace half of U.S. imports, and redirect to our domestic economy $350 billion that currently goes to foreign crude (half the previously noted $700 billion allocated to foreign crude oil).

Consider these employment statistics related to our oil proposal. The Trans-Alaskan Pipeline System project created 70,000 new jobs while it was built between 1975 and 1977. The current Alaska Natural Gas Pipeline project to bring natural gas from Prudhoe Bay to the Midwestern U.S. states created 2,000 new jobs in the early planning stages, and will add another 9,000 workers as production ramps-up. Between 1980 and 1994, $22.5 billion was spent on projects in Alaska's North Slope oil fields, creating over 30,000 new jobs. In addition, 78% of the specific product and supplies procurement for this project went to states such as Texas ($6.8 billion), California ($3.2 billion), and Washington ($1.7 billion) in support of the infrastructure, resulting in another 14,000 new jobs in those states. During the summer 2010 oil clean-up of the British Petroleum offshore platform in the Gulf of Mexico, the Obama Administration reported that 23,000 secondary related jobs would be lost to just a short-term moratorium on drilling. (Mark Tapscott, *Obama Knew Drilling Ban Would Cost 23,000 Jobs*, WASHINGTON EXAMINER (August 21, 2010), www.washingtonexaminer.com/opinion/blogs/beltway-

JOB CREATION

confidential/Obama-knew-Gulf-drilling-ban-would-cost-23000-jobs-101220729.html).

Exxon reports that the development of one new refinery typically creates 7,000 immediate new jobs, with another 2,500 workers needed as the facility progresses through coming to full online status. But while the U.S. had on average 300 to 325 refineries nationwide from just after WWII to 1981, their numbers dropped to around 200 in 1990, and under 150 in 2006; the existing 146 facilities are all running at or near capacity and cannot keep up with continued increases in demand for gasoline, heating oil, jet fuel, and related refined products; however, the tremendous advances in clean air and related environmentally friendly technologies developed since 2000 would make new refineries very low on emissions, while being extremely efficient in their production capabilities. (See, *Irving Refinery means 7,000 jobs*, Daily Commercial News and Construction Record (January 29, 2007)http://www.dailycommercialnews.com/article/20070129600; *Green Field Refinery to Create More Than 7,000 Jobs*, CSR West Africa.com (July 29, 2010) http://csrwestafrica.com/2010/07/green-field-refinery-to-create-more-than-7000-jobs/; *Bayelsa Refinery to Create 7,000 Jobs*, The Nation (July 23, 2010) http://thenationonlineng.net/web3/mobile/news/6811.html; *Iraq to Build 2.5bn Misan Refinery*, AMEInfo.com (March 23, 2009) http://www.ameinfo.com/189573.html; *HPCL To Continue Expansion Programme With 360,000b/d Maharashtra Refinery*, Penn Energy (December 1, 2010) www.pennenergy.com/index/articles/newsdisplay/1308613128.html; Perry, M. J., University of Michigan, Flint Economics and Finance blogspot (June 2, 2008) http://mjperry.blogspot.com/2008/06/no-new-oil-refineries-since-1976.html).

A *Wharton Econometrics* report on developing ANWR concluded that 736,000 new jobs would be created by exploration, development, production, distribution, and related infrastructure capital investments in the project. Primary job creation would

JOB CREATION

include: 225,000 workers in skilled trades, 145,000 in support services, 135,000 in general construction, and 128,000 in manufacturing among the top four categories. Secondary job creation is projected to impact more than 35 other states which would fulfill thousands of related product and service contracts. The ripple effect would be significant, not only for primary and secondary job creation, but also for steadying and even reducing oil prices in the longer term, and providing additional fuel to support economic growth, while providing additional strategic safeguards for future U.S. energy supplies. (ANWR Could Create 736,000 Jobs, by Arctic Power. (*ANWR Could Create 736,000 Jobs*, by Arctic Power (ANWR Information Brief, February 1, 2001) http://www.anwr.org/features /pdfs/employment-facts.pdf).

Domestic oil supply and production is necessary to encourage sustained economic growth, protect our national interests from undue foreign influence, keep our oil revenues in the U.S. and bridge the gap between our current energy needs and the availability of economically viable sources of clean energy. Continued efforts to curtail the domestic supply and production of fossil fuels places both our national security and economic interests at sever risk while creating uncertainty in the business community discouraging growth and job creation.

Realistic Projections from Increased Certainty

Should the government choose to follow our advice that it stop creating fear and uncertainty in the business community and immediately act to create certainty and a business friendly environment, the easiest prediction to make is that such actions would release the currently pent up energy of the free enterprise system leading to dynamic economic growth and meaningful job creation. Once government decides that economic prosperity, rather than an ideological social agenda, is its top priority, the steps it need to take are straightforward. All that is currently

JOB CREATION

missing is the commitment and the political courage necessary to initiate the process. First, do no harm. Eliminate, modify, or suspend the current legislative and regulatory agenda that encompasses initiatives such as nationalizing health insurance (a goal already accomplished but yet to be implemented), creating a Cap and Trade energy economy, and imposing Card Check unionization on the business community. Then, initiate a positive agenda where government moves to the sidelines and lets the free enterprise system function. Our four positive action proposals encompass tax reductions, conducting a cost benefits analysis of our current regulatory system with the goal of meaningfully reducing regulation, reducing the size of government, and creating confidence in our energy supply by increasing our domestic oil production as we develop alternative energy sources.

With respect to our first proposal for positive action, there are dozens of realistic permutations of how government could implement tax cuts while also eliminating certain taxes. Our intent is not to examine each viable configuration and argue the merits of one scheme versus another. But the first proposal to cut taxes across-the-board in the eight categories noted in subchapter 9.31 above would immediately signal a strengthening of *The Certainty Factor*. While we recognize that cutting and eliminating taxes, and drastically reducing the size and complexity of the tax code and the burden of compliance would have an initial negative impact on professionals in the tax preparation and related tax-law industries, the net effect would prove to be very positive. Individuals and companies would have significantly more discretionary funds available for purchases, investments, R+D, savings, and modernizing technology and infrastructure. Our analysis finds that our first proposal will produce a net increase of between 800,000 and 1.1 million new jobs in the private sector (even after factoring out job losses due to lower taxes and simplified compliance), while saving taxpayers at least $300 billion *annually* over the first three to five years.

JOB CREATION

The cost of our current regulatory framework ($1.75 trillion or 14% of national income in 2008 and certainly meaningfully higher today) is unreasonable, unsustainable and unnecessary. We are getting benefits, both financial and social, well below the amount we are spending. The negative impact of the overregulation on business is difficult to measure but is unquestionably very significant. A moratorium on new regulations while we conduct an independent bipartisan cost-benefits analysis with the goal of reducing regulation to a reasonable level will not result in immediate regulatory reduction, it will at least signal to the business community that the government is aware of the problem, will refrain from unreasonably further expanding the regulatory structure and is committed to reducing both regulations and the bureaucracy that has grow to an enormous size around them. On its own, this could strengthen *The Certainty Factor* and well lead to immediate job creation.

The third proposal, to dramatically reduce government spending across the board, and eliminate certain spending programs altogether, would also strengthen *The Certainty Factor.* Just as the first proposal would have an initial negative impact on tax preparation and tax law related jobs in that industry, we also recognize that many long-established government programs would be negatively impacted in the initial one-to-three years as many government jobs are scaled back or eliminated. However, the government could phase these jobs out over time combined with normal expected attrition, normal retirement, and early retirement. Federal, state, and local government budgets will all have to be reduced in relative synch with each other. There will certainly be an initial backlash from both the proposed cuts in spending and the civil servant and related jobs that go with those cuts. But look at the alternative: As noted above, The Bureau of Labor Statistics reports that from 2009 to 2010, the federal government added 86,000 permanent (non-census) jobs to the rolls - and high-paying jobs at that. The number of federal salaries over $100,000 per year has increased by nearly 50% since the

JOB CREATION

beginning of the 2008 recession. Today, the average federal worker earns 77% more than the average private-sector worker, according to a USA Today analysis of data from the federal Office of Personnel Management. Our analysis concludes that a decisive ten percent cut in spending in the first year, followed by three years of additional five percent annual cuts, would result in a 22.8% aggregate drop in overall government spending. This would put $550-$600 billion per year back to the private sector, and produce a net increase of 3.6 million new jobs in the first four years of reduced federal budgets. This allows for total government employment reductions that will be a direct result of scaled back and eliminated federal programs, entitlements, subsidies, and other mandatory and discretionary spending.

The fourth proposal, to aggressively expand domestic oil production, would set very positive expectations for virtually all domestic enterprise regarding future opportunities for controlling costs, expanding operations, improving profits, and building wealth. Individuals would also experience a stronger *Certainty Factor* regarding expected gains in personal and household incomes, which would translate into optimism about consumer spending, savings, investments, home improvements, and other discretionary purchases. Our analysis concludes that lifting the Congressional ban on offshore drilling to begin new exploration, building new refineries nationwide, and opening up a relatively tiny subdivision of the northern sectors of ANWR for exploration and development would collectively result in creating between 2.1 million and 2.4 million new jobs in the first 12-18 months, and add another 1.3 million new jobs out to the end of the fourth year.

Over the course of about five years, we project that these four proposals would create between 5.9 million and 8.4 million net new primary and close-in proximate jobs throughout the private sector. Having examined employment multipliers calculated on more than a dozen industries over the last two decades, a very

JOB CREATION

conservative aggregate multiplier of just 1.25 would increase that net job creation to between 7.4 million and 10.5 million. Considering there are currently about 155 million total workers in the U.S. labor market, if the ranks of the unemployed dropped by the lower end of that projected range (say, 8.2 million new jobs), it would translate to 5.23 percentage points of reduced unemployment, such that the late 2010 levels of around 14.9 million out of work and a near 10% unemployment rate would improve to just under 7 million out of work and a national unemployment rate of 4.3% - about where it was in the early 2000s during the Bush Administration's first term. These new jobs would NOT be tax *consuming* government supported jobs, but tax *generating* jobs that would create new revenues for government, even while being taxed at lower rates and on fewer bases. We project the salaries and wages to these new positions will exceed $370 billion annually and contribute $200 billion in total new personal and corporate tax revenues to the federal government over the course of the first five years.

We also strongly recommend that the president and the Washington political elites stop bashing business every chance they get. The administration's continued negative remarks about market opportunities, pricing, and profits set the tone for disregarding, and even crippling, *The Certainty Factor.* A vibrant and dynamic private sector IS the primary catalyst for robust, sustainable job creation. The private sector salaries and wages paid to individuals, and operating profits generated by companies, are the tax revenue-generating sources of the government's funding. Even a self-absorbed elite career politician without any business experience, who is clueless about the core principles of micro- and macro-economics, has to acknowledge that there is no government without a fully functioning private sector. While businesses view revenue as products and services sold to end-users at competitive prices, government's revenue is simply the taxes, fees, tariffs, and other charges it imposes on individuals and businesses, so it should clearly follow that politicians would want

JOB CREATION

the private sector to be as strong as possible to ensure the sustainability of that tax-revenue source of funds. Demonizing mergers, acquisitions, joint ventures, global partnerships, cross-border labor and manufacturing, and of course strong profits sends a clear negative signal to American private enterprise and individual households. Instead, politicians should do everything they can to embrace and support U.S. businesses as their partners in building and maintaining a vibrant economy and reliable tax-base. By making statements that attack businesses and question the underlying philosophy of profits and private wealth creation, government actually undermines its own funding source. It's time for government to proudly stand alongside businesses and individuals, and do everything it can to promote a positive economic outlook that supports strong market growth and profits.

In the end, it is time to replace what has proven time and again to NOT work in the US economy, with policies that DO work, and HAVE worked, in creating new jobs. Higher taxes on individuals and companies have never promoted job creation or spurred growth in the economy. A recent study examined anti-recession programs in the last fifty years, and found that each program the government enacted it implemented far too late. This was due to policy makers failing to recognize the recession until well after it hit and programs taking too long to work. "Stimulus packages have typically taken effect after the economy is already turning around. The result of these [supposed] stimulants [tends to be] more inflation instead of more job growth." (Bruce Bartlett, *Why Isn't The Stimulus Stimulating?*, FORBES (June 26, 2009), http://www.forbes.com/2009/06/25/stimulus-obama-keynes-opinions-columnists-bruce-bartlett.html).

Stimulus is probably the wrong metaphor to remedy our economy. "Rather than getting jazzed up, we need to be calmed down and to take the time to learn from the Great Depression, a time when government did too much, not too little." (James K. Glassman, *Stimulus: A History of Folly*, COMMENTARY Magazine (March 1,

2009), http://www. commentarymagazine.com/printarticle.cfm/stimulus--a-history-of-folly-14953). "Political systems and their leaders often prove hesitant to take dramatic action on the sort of partial evidence available when a threat is emerging, avoiding decisions on controversial and expensive measures until there is no choice." That quote, originally written about Europe, now also applies to the United States; for all the talk of bold leadership and change, President Obama's contribution to addressing Americans' ballooning national debt problem is first to make it much worse, [as his] spending explosion [will] lead the U.S. to the same course as Greece" (J.D. Foster, *Still Not Greece, but Getting Closer Every Day*, THE FOUNDRY (June 27, 2010), http://blog.heritage.org/2010/06/17/still-not-greece-but-getting-closer-every-day/).

It's time now for strong leadership in the U.S., not toward the Greek model of burgeoning debt, consistently high unemployment, a bankrupt nationalized health care system, civil servant pensions valued at over half the country's GDP, and a habitually stifled economy, but toward the tried and true tenets of American private enterprise. Opportunities for sustained gains on individual and business endeavors, strong profit potential due to low taxes and scaled back government intervention, and the prospects for creating and retaining wealth – these hallmarks of the private sector and free markets built this great nation and the world's most successful economy. It's time to do everything we can to support a strong *Certainty Factor* about the future economic environment, so that businesses will begin investing in their future prospects and creating jobs.

JOB CREATION

Chapter 10

Three Added Benefits of Successful Job Creation

*"The great dialectic in our time is not,
as anciently and by some still supposed,
between capital and labor -
it is between economic enterprise and the state."*

- John Kenneth Galbraith
Economist

We will conclude with a brief overview of three additional benefits that accrue to the private sector economy as a result of this type of successful job creation. The first added benefit is based on the work of Arthur Laffer, and his insights into an interesting phenomenon about the relationship between government tax revenues and marginal tax rates. The second added benefit connects a direct extension of new job creation to the U.S. capital markets. The third added benefit is quite provocative, because great job creation so strengthens *The Certainty Factor* that it actually helps to create even more jobs for the economy due to sustained positive expectations throughout the private sector.

More Tax Revenues – Lessons From Laffer

Why is it so hard to connect the proverbial dots between tax policies and economic performance? Lower taxes provide an incentive for business development and job creation, while higher

JOB CREATION

taxes are a disincentive for business activity and severely curtail new jobs. Our *Certainty Factor* - covered in detail throughout the book - *improves* dramatically when local, state, and federal governments reduce taxes AND reduce spending. More funds then remain in the private sector and businesses have greater incentives to pursue innovation, R+D, expansion, and sustainable profits – all of which always lead to increased job creation. Arthur Laffer is best known for his advocacy of "supply side" economics while advising the Reagan Administration. His now famous "Laffer Curve" provides a system to examine how much total tax revenue a government would collect across a range of tax rates between zero percent (0%) and 100% - the logic being that at zero percent government obviously does not collect any taxes from the private sector, and at 100% government also does not collect any taxes, because at that rate all incentive to produce taxable income is entirely removed because all income must be paid to the government. Somewhere between the two ends of the scale there is an optimum point at which a tax rate is both low enough to spur economic activity (providing sufficient optimism to pursue growth and profits due to a strong *Certainty Factor)*, and yet high enough to generate strong total tax revenues for the government. The conclusion is that a relatively lower tax rate will maximize the private sector's incentives for economic growth while also bringing in maximum tax revenue to the Treasury. This translates into a larger aggregate economy, that when taxed at a lower overall tax rate, will actually produce more tax revenue than a smaller economy taxed at a higher rate. And of course, the former scenario recognizes that this lower relative tax rate is actually a prime driver of the larger, growing economy. A simple example would be a $15 trillion economy taxed at a 20% net effective rate produces $3 trillion in tax revenue. But if the rate was lowered to 18%, which helps the economy grow over time to $17.5 trillion, that would generate $3.15 trillion in tax revenue (a five percent increase), even though the tax rate has dropped by ten percent.

JOB CREATION

Numerous studies have shown with clear empirical data that states with lower taxes have stronger economies and lower unemployment, while states with higher taxes have weaker economies, huge budget deficits, and the highest unemployment rates in the country (See CATO INSTITUTE, http://www.Cato.org; U.S. DEPT. OF THE TREASURY, http://www.USTreas.gov; CTR. ON BUDGET AND POLICY PRIORITIES, http://www.cbpp.org; NAT'L CTR. FOR POLICY ANALYSIS, http://www.ncpa.org). Laffer has succinctly noted that when taxes are increased, "People can change the volume, the location, and the composition of their income, and they can do so in response to changes in government policies, so it shouldn't surprise anyone that the nine states without an income tax are growing far faster and attracting more people than are the nine states with the highest income tax rates; people and [firms] change the location of income based on incentives." (Arthur Laffer, *Tax Hikes and the 2011 Economic Collapse*, WALL STREET JOURNAL (June 6, 2010), http://online.wsj.com/article/SB10001424052748704113504575264513748386610.html) ("Laffer Tax Hikes Article").

This speaks directly to *The Certainty Factor*, as higher tax rates reduce certainty about future business opportunities. Higher taxes also reduce incentives to be profitable and build wealth because the government will confiscate more through taxation. Firms change states, and even countries, to lower their corporate and individual tax liabilities. In 2009, Texas Governor Rick Perry said it best, "Our state is competing with Germany, France, Japan, and China [so] we'd better have a pro-growth tax system or those American jobs will be out-sourced." (Arthur Laffer & Stephen Moore, *Soak the Rich, Lose the Rich*, WALL STREET JOURNAL (May 18, 2009), http://online.wsj.com/article/SB124260067214828295.html). The evidence is clear. Texas has a business-friendly, low-tax environment, and from 2000 to 2008 "created more jobs than all the other states combined . . . ." (K. White, *The EPA's Anti-Prosperity Agenda*, Texas Policy Foundation (October 18, 2010) www.texaspolicy.com/ commentaries_single.php?report_id=3338).

JOB CREATION

"Massive spending in the 1930s, 1960s, and 1970s all failed to increase economic growth rates. Yet in the 1980s and 1990s - when the federal government shrank by one-fifth as a percentage of GDP, the U.S. economy enjoyed its greatest expansion to date." (Brian Riedl, *Why Government Spending Does Not Stimulate Economic Growth*, HERITAGE FOUNDATION (June 16, 2010), www.heritage.org/research/reports/2010 /01/why-government-spending-does-not-stimulate-economic-growth-answering-the-critics). The 1921 U.S. unemployment rate was nearly 12%, but instead of implementing stimulus spending with increased debt and new taxes, Presidents Harding and Coolidge cut taxes and federal spending, and unemployment dropped to 3.3 percent, and the U.S. enjoyed budget surpluses throughout the 1920s. Then, in contrast, during the 1930s, President Hoover's federal stimulus for banks, railroads, and the farm industry helped create a huge jump in unemployment to almost 25%. (Burt Folsom, *Comparing the Great Depression to the Great Recession*, THE FREEMAN (June, 2010), www.thefreemanonline.org/ columns/our-economic-past/comparing-the-great-depression-to-the-great-recession/).

In 1981, President Reagan (with bipartisan support) began the first phase in a series of tax cuts passed under the Economic Recovery Tax Act (ERTA). The bulk of the cuts didn't take effect until January 1, 1983. Reagan's delayed tax cuts were the mirror image of today's delayed tax rate *increases* set for 2011 and 2012. During 1981 and 1982, businesses and individuals deferred so much economic activity that real GDP was basically flat (no growth), and the unemployment rate rose to well over 10%. But right at the tax boundary of January 1, 1983 the US economy took off like a rocket, with *real* growth reaching 7.5% in 1983 and 5.5% in 1984. (Laffer Tax Hikes Article).

So why is the current administration planning to allow certain tax cuts to expire? While Laffer clearly gets it right on the impact of tax reductions on the economy, that same principle also holds true for the negative effects of proposed tax increases. He notes that "if people know tax rates will be higher next year than they are this year, what will those people do this year? They will shift production and income out of next year into this year, and as a result, income this year has already been inflated above where it otherwise should be and next year (2011) income will be lower than it otherwise should be". He continues, "the prospect of rising prices, higher interest rates, and more regulations [in 2011] will further entice demand and supply to be shifted into 2010 - a major reason that the economy in 2010 has appeared [stronger] as it has; however, when we pass the tax boundary of January 1, 2011, we [could] get our worst nightmare of a severe *double dip recession*" (See: Laffer Tax Hikes Article).

It seems logical that if lower taxes mean more money in the hands of individuals and businesses in the private sector - money they can invest, spend, and save - then raising taxes in 2011 and 2012 will harm the economy. High taxes are a clear *disincentive* to make money, many individuals and companies will pursue strategies to *lower* their incomes in the coming years in order to pay less tax. In addition, many firms will look to move their primary locations outside the U.S. to countries with more favorable tax rates.

"Reaganomics [tax cuts were] so successful that it all but abolished the business cycle for a generation [as] the economy took off at the end of 1982 on a 25-year economic boom interrupted by only two, short, shallow recessions in 1990-1991 and 2001. That is why today we no longer recognize the natural workings of the business cycle" (Peter Ferrara, *The Coming Crash of 2011*, The American Spectator- February 10, 2010, www.spectator.org/archives/2010/02/10/the-coming-crash-of-2011/print). Laffer warns: "people don't realize the damage [tax increases] do because they are delayed; but once put in place, [income] taxes will reach an all time high, and unemployment and deficit numbers will make the current ones seem reasonable" (See: Laffer Tax Hike Article).

JOB CREATION

Higher taxes translate not only into a worsening unemployment situation, but also larger federal budget deficits, more total debt, and subsequently higher interest rates and inflation. Companies will have less profit (retained earnings) to invest in new equipment, machinery, physical space, and R+D. Individuals will have less to spend on home improvements, vacations, new cars, and other durable goods.

All of the additional federal borrowing needed for government programs also increases the nation's short-term money supply. A subsequent Laffer report clearly demonstrated how exacerbated the increase in the money supply had become through April 2009. The report showed the annual percentage increase in the money supply since the onset of the 2008 recession, where from 1961-2007 the annual percentage change in the monetary base never rose more than 20% (even at the Y2K and 9/11 spikes), but jumped 128% in less than 18 months through December 2010 (Art Laffer, *Laffer Associates Economic Outlook: 2010 And Beyond*, www.tn.gov/finance/newsrel/Documents/Laffer.pdf). He comments on this process noting, "the expansion in the nation's money supply will then be responsible for inflation and higher interest rates, both of which will further reduce the opportunities for job creation, as products and services become more expensive, and the costs go up to secure various loans." (Arthur Laffer, *Get Ready For Inflation and Higher Interest Rates*, WALL STREET JOURNAL (June 8, 2009), http://online.wsj.com/article/SB124458888993599879.html). The decrease in money demand and the increase in monetary growth will absolutely lead to increased inflation and higher interest rates. The higher interest rates will then further reduce the demand for money, which puts even greater inflationary pressure on prices in the economy.

But reduced federal spending combined with lower tax rates produces the opposite effect in the economy. With less government borrowing, the money supply does not expand, and inflation and interest rates remain low, both of which increase the

JOB CREATION

full range of capital availability and investment opportunities for job creation, as prices on products and services remain stable, and strong business profits help keep the demand for new loans relatively lower, so the costs of borrowing also remain low.

More Capital and Lower Costs of Capital

The second additional benefit of successful job creation is that increased business profits, and higher individual and household incomes, always translate into more savings and investment, as the private sector diversifies its holdings across both the money market and the capital market. When the private sector is thriving, it increases the overall capital availability in short-term credit and money markets, as well as longer-term debt and equity markets. This results in easing capital access and a wide range of funding for additional economic growth which increases the supply of funds available helping bring down the costs of capital for businesses and individuals.

As the number of individuals with jobs increases so do personal incomes. An increase in personal income results in increased individual spending, savings, and investment. By spending, individuals increase profits for the businesses whose products or services they purchase further driving economic prosperity. As cash is a depreciating asset, businesses with increased profits or cash flow are inherently incentivized to make capital expenditures to further grow their businesses. If done prudently, such investments further the investing company's business and result in further direct and concentric circle jobs creation. Individuals with excess cash may also increase their savings for the short-term and invest for the longer-term by purchasing equity in companies they believe will grow, or by purchasing bonds, which makes additional debt financing available to the business community. Such investments increase the cash available for capital improvements and growth in the private sector. While depositing funds in a bank is hardly a high return investment,

JOB CREATION

doing so also increases the working capital available to businesses that borrow from those banks. As such, by increasing individual incomes, job creation has the added benefit of enhancing the cash available in the capital markets for investment, or reinvestment, by the firms that require capital for growth. This continues to fund sustainable growth. The result is both growth for existing businesses and the creation of more new businesses funded by venture capital lending, "angel" money, private equity firms, and traditional lending institutions that now have more capital to lend. Notably, all this is accomplished without government support through taxpayer dollars.

When profits and income are strong, it helps reduce the overall demand for outside capital, as companies and individuals have more internally-generated funds providing a good starting point from which to make short-term expenditures and long-term investments. Firms can do short-term inventory and accounts receivable funding internally due to strong working capital and positive operating cash flow. Individuals and households are less likely to use credit card debt for short-term purchases and balancing monthly cash flow because disposable income is reliable and sustainable, and expected to grow as the economy continues to expand. Firms can also do more of their longer-term equipment, machinery, infrastructure, and technology purchases internally through retained earnings as a result of strong profits. These all work together to reduce demand for outside funds, which helps lower the pricing of intermediary capital.

On the supply side of the markets, financial intermediaries such as commercial banks, have increased deposits, cash flow, and working capital to support short-term transactions in the money market, so the supply of short-term capital is up. Other financial firms such as investment banks and institutional investors, also have stronger equity value positions to support longer-term transactions in the capital market, so similarly, their supply of longer-term capital is also good. Given the relatively lower

JOB CREATION

demand by firms and individuals for both short-term working capital in the money market, and longer-term debt and equity funding in the capital market, and the higher supply of short-term and long-term capital availability, the overall costs of obtaining outside capital will decrease as a result of robust job creation and its accompanying positive *Certainty Factor*. This translates into lower costs for short-term loans on current assets and the carrying costs of accounts payable. It also reduces the costs of longer-term borrowing through both commercial bank loans and the issuing of corporate bonds. Finally, the cost of obtaining longer-term equity capital for IPOs, mergers, and acquisitions will also be lower. These lower costs of capital reduce the intrinsic risk associated with growth and expansion plans. A strong *Certainty Factor* makes future sales and profit forecasts more reliable, and improves expectations. The lower cost of capital also improves the present values of proposed capital investment projects, which increases owners' equity.

Even More Jobs

It is well worth noting that while improved tax revenues, more capital access, and lower costs of capital are welcome additional benefits of successful job creation, another great benefit is that over time, sustainable job creation further strengthens *The Certainty Factor*, supporting positive expectations about market growth and future profits, which result in *even more jobs being added to the economy* - a residual outcome of sustained economic prosperity. It works very simply like this. The reduced risk and improved expectations of a strong *Certainty Factor* provide the optimism and impetus for businesses and entrepreneurs to pursue growth opportunities and the corresponding higher sales and profits that come with those endeavors. To make this growth happen, businesses and entrepreneurs create job to do all the increased work resulting in primary job creation within the firm and in close proximity to the primary employment. Secondary job creation extends out to the tangent markets, industries, and

JOB CREATION

communities across a wide range of vendors, distributors, service and support, and infrastructure-related expansion as concentric circles around the primary hiring.

With reduced government regulations and lower taxes, firms realize improved profits and cash flow, and individuals receive more income. These increase the supply of short-term and long-term capital and reduce relative demand for capital by firms and individuals. The resulting lower costs of capital provide even further strengthening of *The Certainty Factor*, and firms and individuals continue to pursue even more market opportunities for growth, profits, and wealth creation. This "second wave" of optimism results in businesses and entrepreneurs creating even more jobs beyond the new hiring that occurred in the previous round of expansion.

Sustainable job creation is always possible in the private sector, given the positive economic conditions necessary to support a continued strong *Certainty Factor* and optimism about market opportunities and prospects for growth. Our four proposals for cutting taxes, reducing regulation and government spending, and expanding all aspects of domestic energy production will definitely reduce the uncertain economic climate that has prevailed since the Fall of 2008. Improved positive expectations about the future will incentivize the private sector and job creation will happen on both the primary and secondary levels. In addition, no more government stimulus spending plans, a repeal of government legislation to take control of the health care industry and an end to the pursuit of an economically destructive ideologically based political agenda will further reduce uncertainty and inject new optimism throughout the private sector. Job creation will then move forward, and with it, government will likely see improved tax revenues coming in from both individuals and businesses (even with lower tax rates). Combined with significant reductions in spending, the government

JOB CREATION

can balance the federal budget or bring it into surplus. Capital availability will improve and ultimately result in lower costs of capital for individuals and companies. This pro-private sector climate will further strengthen *The Certainty Factor* and result in second and third waves of additional new hiring. But at the heart of this plan, government must be herded back into its place, out of the center and onto the sidelines of American private enterprise.

Tom Toles' political cartoon in the June 26, 2010 *Washington Post* nails the current administration's problems directly on the head. The U.S. economy is personified as driving the "recovery" wagon, with a typical American worker hitched to the cart's rigging with a bit in his mouth, but sitting down and unable to pull the cart forward. The economy holds a carrot [incentive] inscribed with "JOBS" out over the worker's head, who has a frustrated dark cloud over his head as the economy comments: "Don't stop now! You almost reached it!" That is the end-all commentary on the failure of government stimulus spending to foster meaningful, lasting recovery. There must be significant job creation. But the private sector cannot get going if the federal government siphons off more and more of the private sector's funds through higher taxes. Yet, for some almost incomprehensible reason, the present administration pursues exactly this "siphoning off" policy.

"Three weeks after taking office, [President Obama] said 'only government has the resources to jolt our economy back into life'. So it follows that he has proposed 'increases in taxes [for 2011] on individual income, capital gains, dividends, inheritances, and risky investments'" (Fred Barnes, *Know-Nothing-In-Chief*, THE WEEKLY STANDARD (August 3, 2009), www.weeklystandard.com/ Content/Public/Articles/000/000/016/765kishz.asp). If the current administration's goal were to incentivize business, create jobs, and foster economic prosperity, high taxes and government growth are neither the rational path nor what has historically proven to be effective. Clearly, the goal can only be an expansion

JOB CREATION

of our federal government beyond anything previously contemplated by most Americans or by our Constitution.

As Galbraith was quoted at the beginning of this chapter: "The great dialectic in our time is not, as anciently and by some still supposed, between capital and labor; it is between economic enterprise and the state." (*Columbia World of Quotations*, Columbia University Press, [1996] http://quotes.dictionary.com/ The_great_dialectic_in_our_time_is_not?). Higher tax rates expand government's power over both the economy and the individual. Lower tax rates generate job creation, economic growth, and prosperity. This really is not all that difficult.

It is relatively easy to understand that one of the benefits of increased job creation will inevitably be increased tax revenue. Obviously, the more vibrant the economy, the more people that are working and have incomes, the more income, sales, corporate, and capital gains taxes people and businesses will pay. If government lowers these tax rates, it will incentivize businesses to grow, thereby increasing the number of people with jobs, which further increases the number of people and businesses paying taxes. If the goal of government is really to increase tax revenues, then job creation and economic prosperity would be the government's primary concern. Increasing tax rates should not be its plan - particularly in a recessionary economy - because increasing tax rates may actually lower tax revenues and retard business growth as noted above.

This was the case during the Carter administration when the top marginal tax rate for individuals was 76%. Not surprisingly, for this and other reasons, the economy went into a severe recessionary decline. As previously noted, in the 1980s a coalition led by President Reagan passed across-the-board tax reductions and immediately upon these reductions taking effect in January of 1983, the economy began a recovery that lasted for nearly two

JOB CREATION

decades. As the economy prospered, we experienced both an increase in employment and an increase in tax revenues despite the lower tax rates. Table 10.1 on the next page summarizes the gains in government tax revenues during the 1980s after tax rates were reduced. As stated by the Heritage Foundation in a 2002 web memo entitled Tax Cuts Increase Federal Revenue: "In 1980, the last year before the [Reagan era] tax cuts, tax revenues were $956 billion (in constant 1996 dollars). Revenues exceeded that 1980 level in eight of the next 10 years, and annual revenues over the next decade averaged $102 billion above the 1980 level (in constant 1996 dollars)." (www.heritage.org/Research/Reports/2002/12/Tax-Cuts-Increase-Federal-Revenues).

Table 10.1

YEAR	TAX REVENUES	INFLATION ADJUSTED	% CHANGE OVER 1980
1980	$956 billion	n/a	n/a

final tax cuts in place at end of 1983

YEAR	TAX REVENUES		
1984	$950 billion	same	same
1985	$1.012 trillion	+ 5.86%	$ 56 billion
1986	$1.035 trillion	+ 8.25%	$ 79 billion
1987	$1.119 trillion	+17.02%	$163 billion
1988	$1.154 trillion	+20.72%	$198 billion
1989	$1.213 trillion	+26.89%	$257 billion
1990	$1.222 trillion	+27.79%	$266 billion
		TOTAL:	**$1.02 trillion**

Source: Heritage Foundation
Compiled and formatted by David Newton

JOB CREATION

Conclusion

The prospects for sustainable job creation can improve dramatically if politicians and the Washington elite will step back from their entrenched thinking that "government knows best" and provide the private sector with the optimistic upside opportunities it needs to start investing its own $2 trillion of cash and other reserves directly into growth plans and creating millions of new jobs.

Now is the time to cut taxes. Politicians must not hesitate on this. Leaving more funds in the hands of private sector businesses and individuals will improve *The Certainty Factor* and increase the prospects for wealth creation. Now is the time to significantly scale back government spending and regulations. Federal budget entitlements can be reworked, scaled back, and/or eliminated and our politicians must not assume otherwise. There is no spending program that can be deemed immune from audit and review. While the short-term pain will require financial adjustments within the economy, the long-term benefits will be well worth it. Now is the time to open wide the immense potential of our domestic oil industry. A well coordinated industry plan that upgrades the U.S. petroleum infrastructure, increases supply and production, reduces risky foreign imports, and utilizes the latest "clean" technologies in a balanced approach to environmental concerns will shore up a significant facet of the U.S. economy while adding millions of new sustainable jobs. The time is now to provide strong vision, leadership, and decision making to lead the U.S. economy back to private sector prosperity.

The current administration would hit an unequivocal "home run" if it decisively reduced its role in the lives of businesses and individuals, and let the time-tested resiliency of the American private enterprise system to do what it does best: Take new venture risks, pursue innovation, invest in R+D and capital assets, modernize and expand infrastructure, and hire new employees to

JOB CREATION

get all that work done. The consumer markets would follow, as would housing and related construction. That is how job creation really works. That is how job creation has always worked. But sadly, government still doesn't "get it." In our vibrant history as a nation of creative entrepreneurs and business owners, there is a vast trove of evidence during times when government DID "get it," and the economy flourished, profits soared, trillions of dollars of new wealth were added to individuals and businesses, and millions of new jobs were created as great new industries and markets opened up on the heels of a strong *Certainty Factor,* based upon optimism and positive expectations. Now is the time for government to "get it" once again, and join the private sector on a clear pathway to economic prosperity. Now is the time!